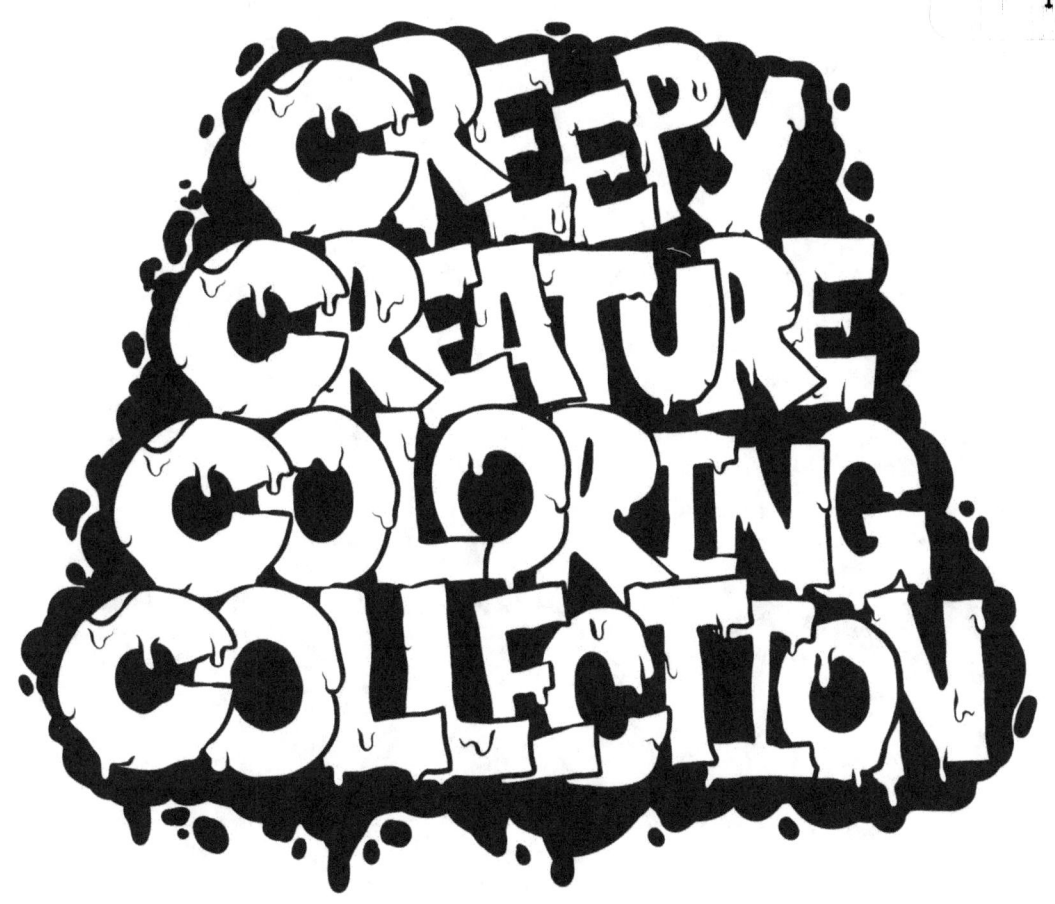

A COLORING BOOK FOR WEIRDOS
BY JAKE PEREZ

SHOW ME WHAT YOU COLORED!
🐦 @JAKEPEREZART
f 📷 @ARTISTJAKEPEREZ

WWW.ARTISTJAKEPEREZ.COM

Copyright © 2020 by Jacob Perez
All rights reserved

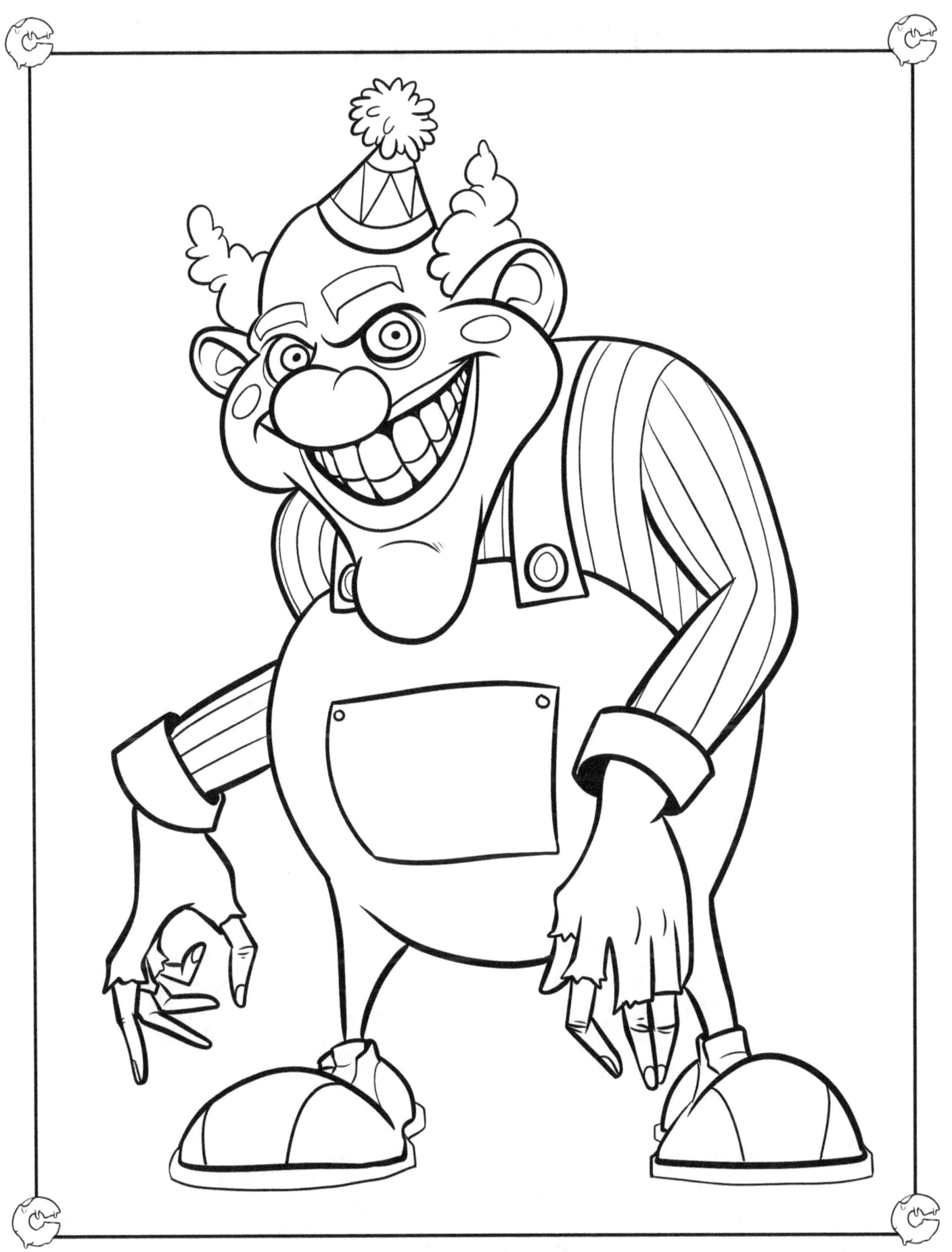

CREEPY CREATURE COLORING COLLECTION

BY JAKE PEREZ

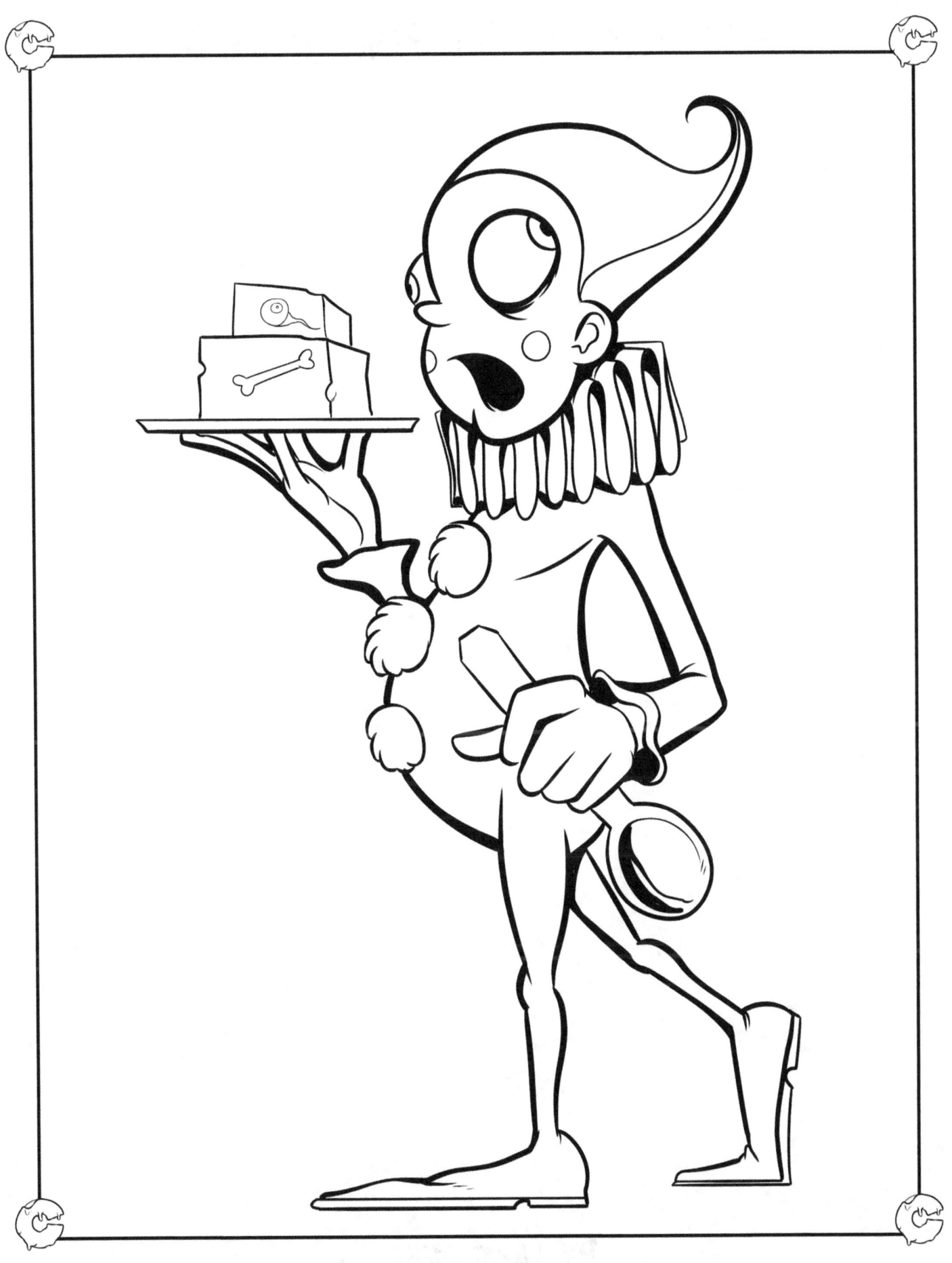

CREEPY CREATURE COLORING COLLECTION

BY JAKE PEREZ

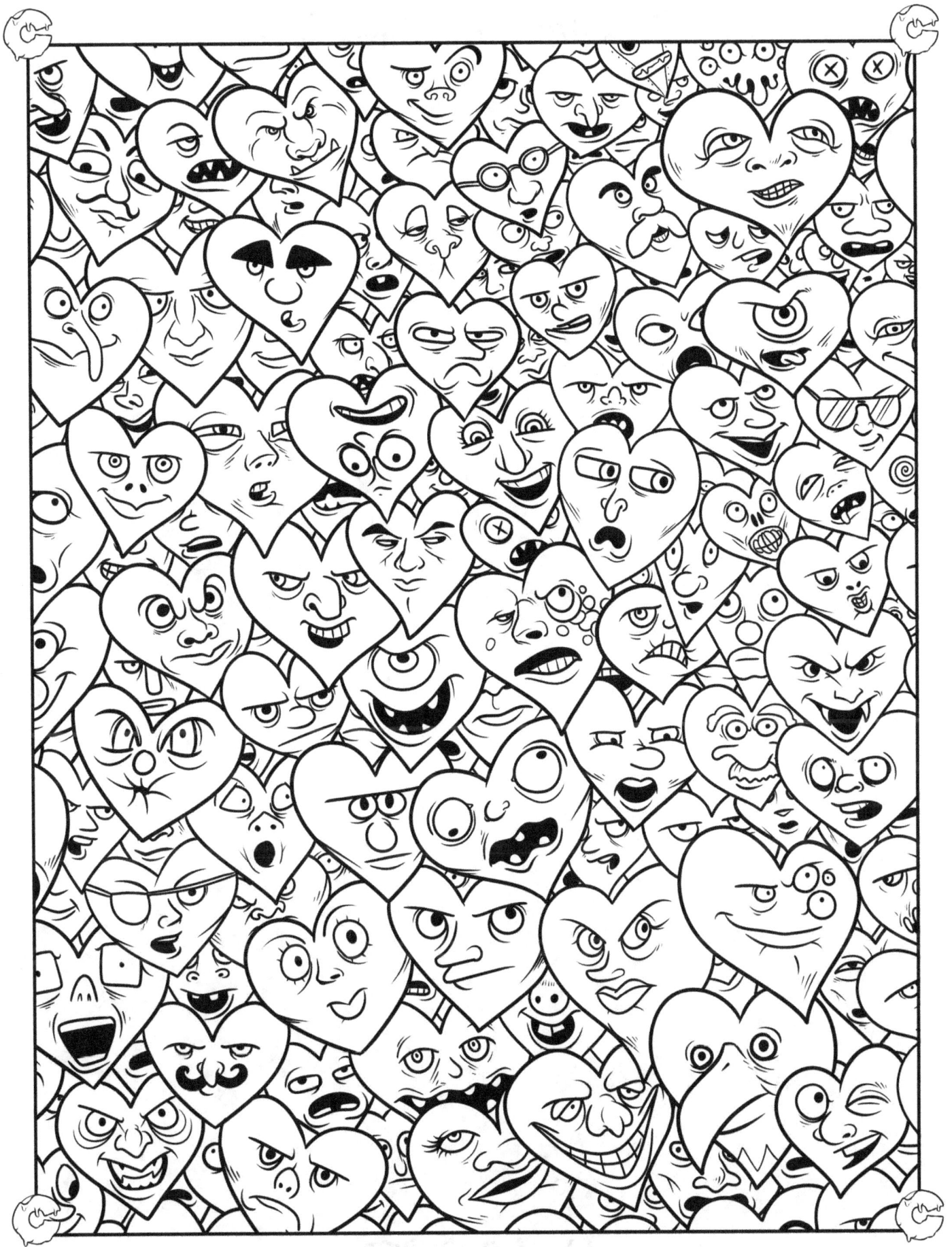

CREEPY CREATURE COLORING COLLECTION

BY JAKE PEREZ

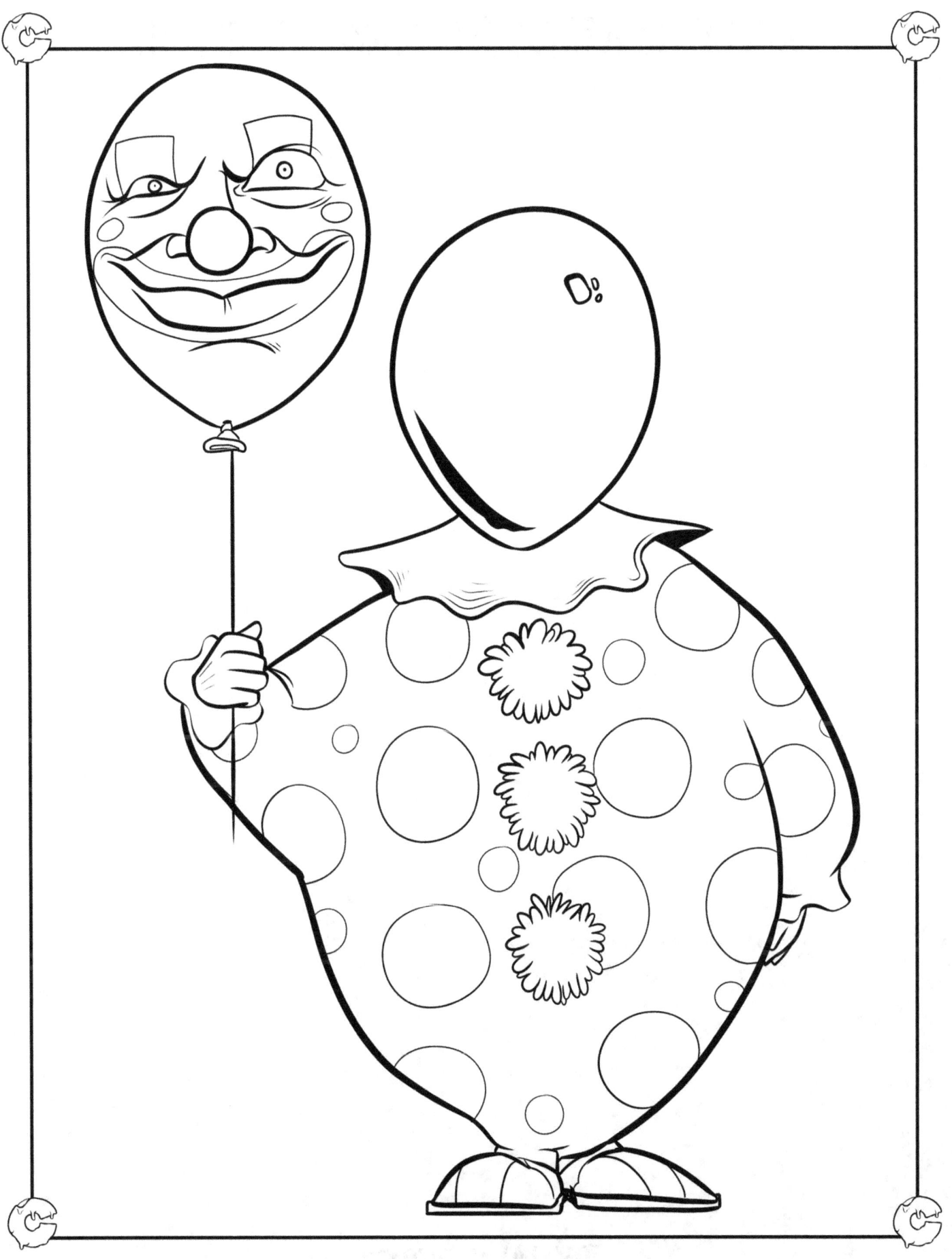

CREEPY CREATURE COLORING COLLECTION

BY JAKE PEREZ

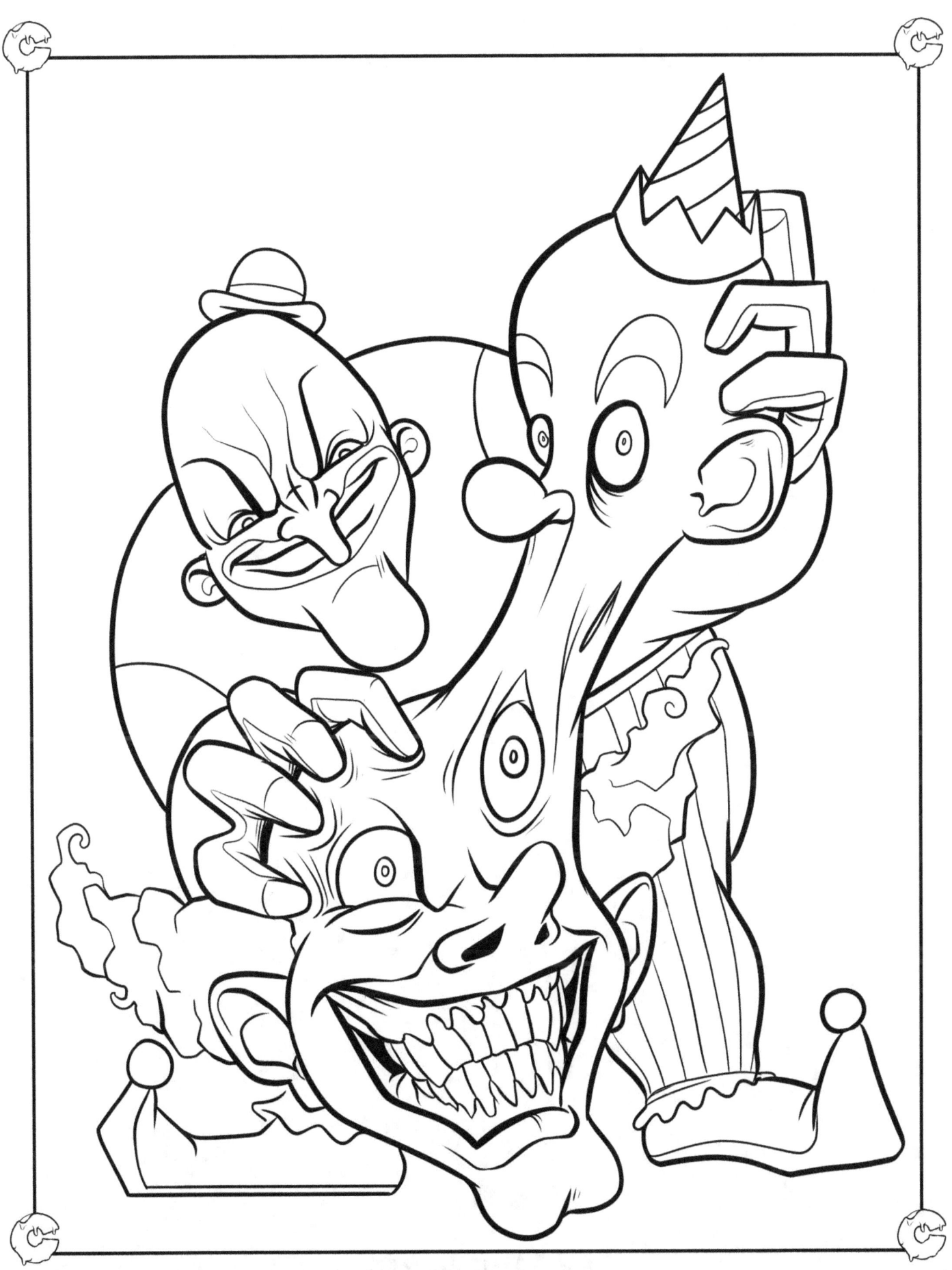

CREEPY CREATURE COLORING COLLECTION

BY JAKE PEREZ

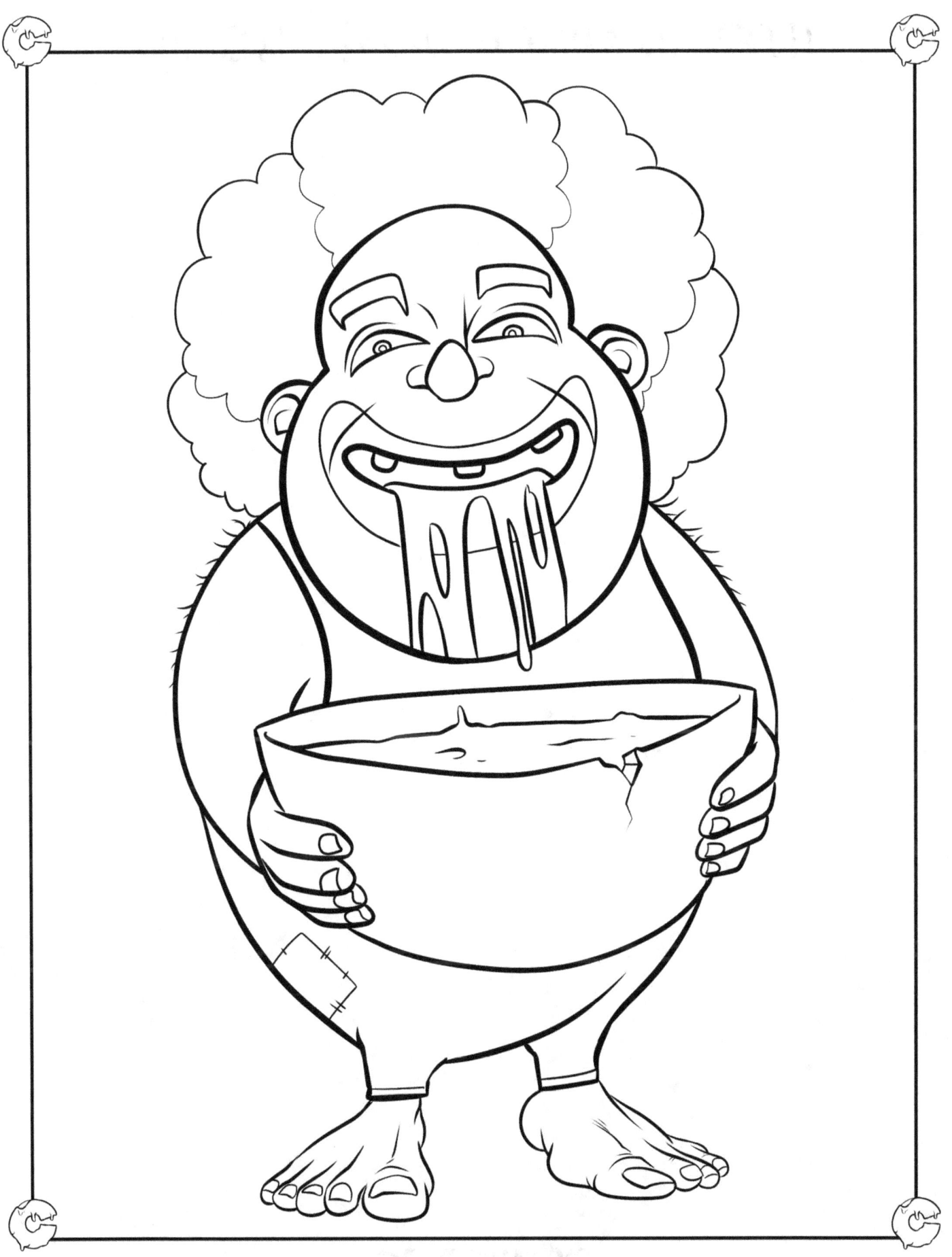

CREEPY CREATURE COLORING COLLECTION

BY JAKE PEREZ

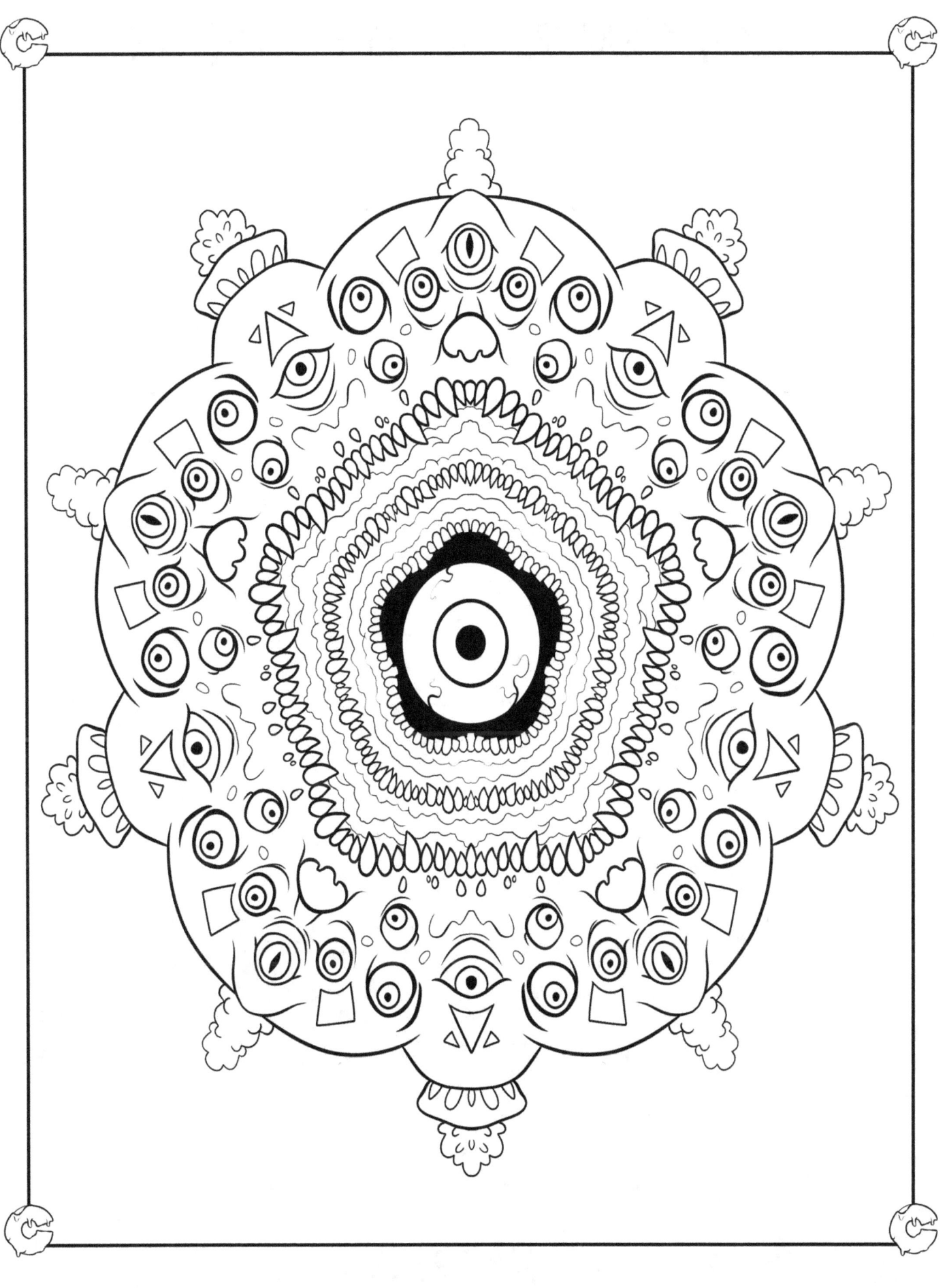

CREEPY CREATURE COLORING COLLECTION

BY JAKE PEREZ

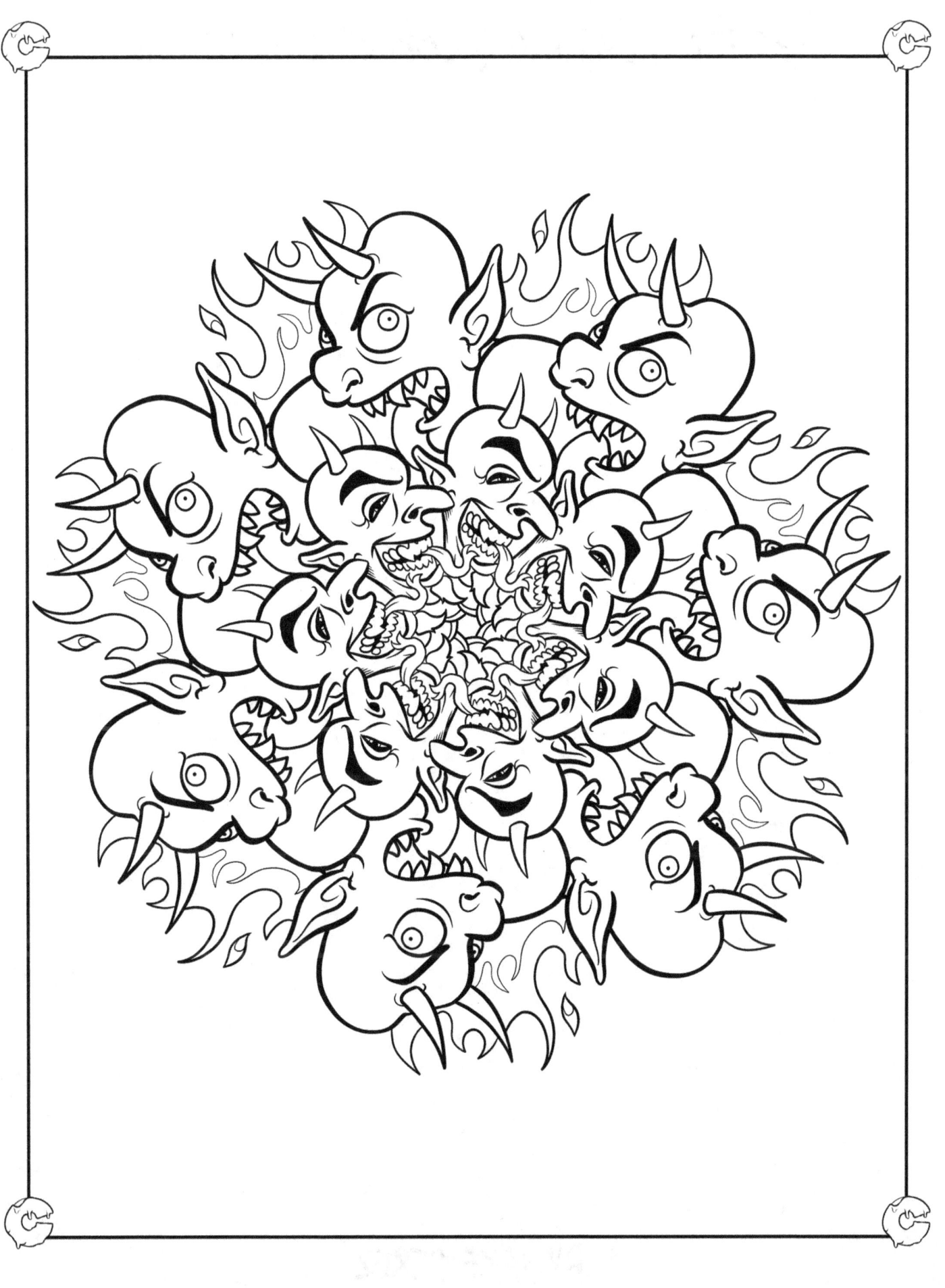

CREEPY CREATURE COLORING COLLECTION

BY JAKE PEREZ

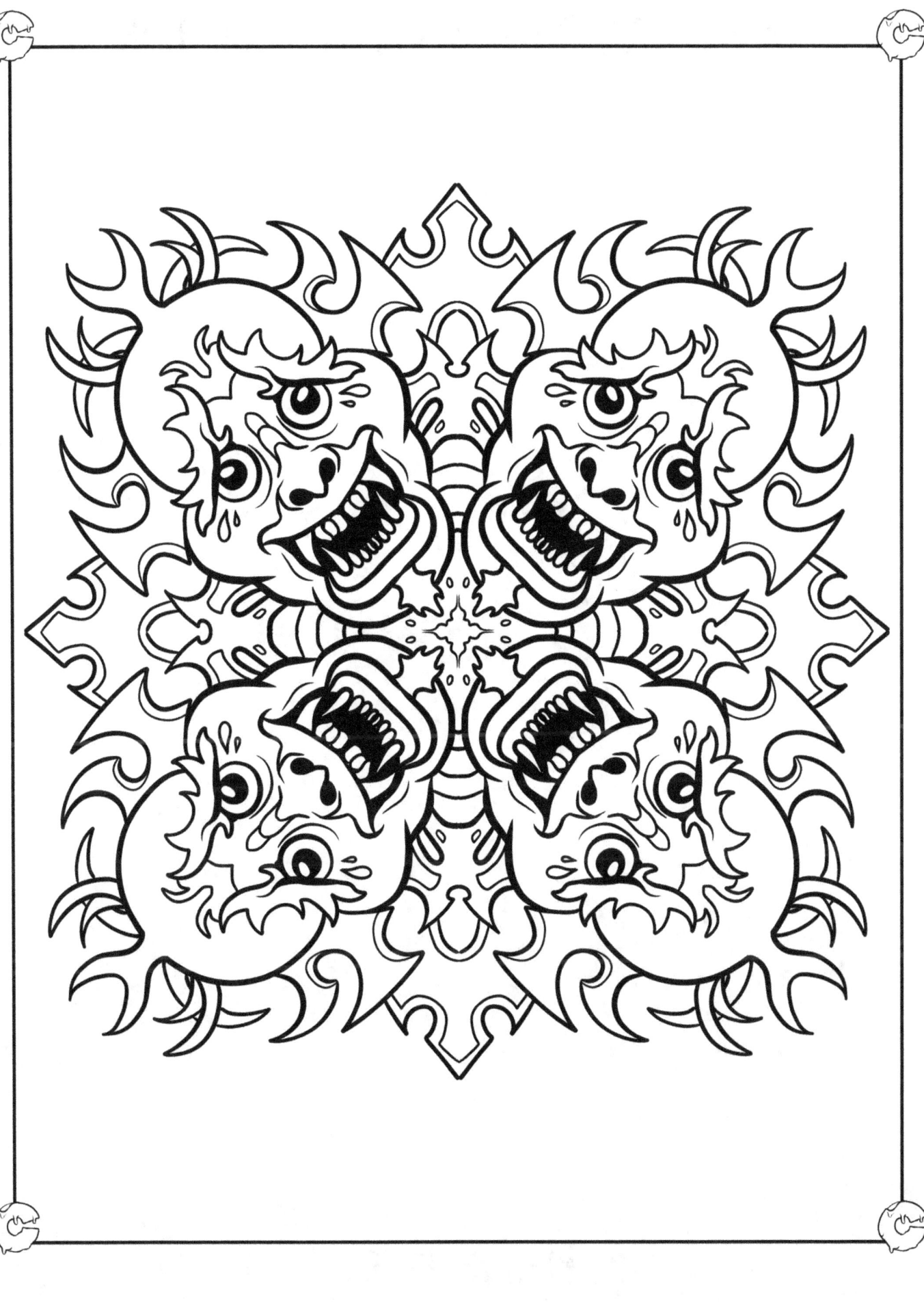

CREEPY CREATURE COLORING COLLECTION

BY JAKE PEREZ

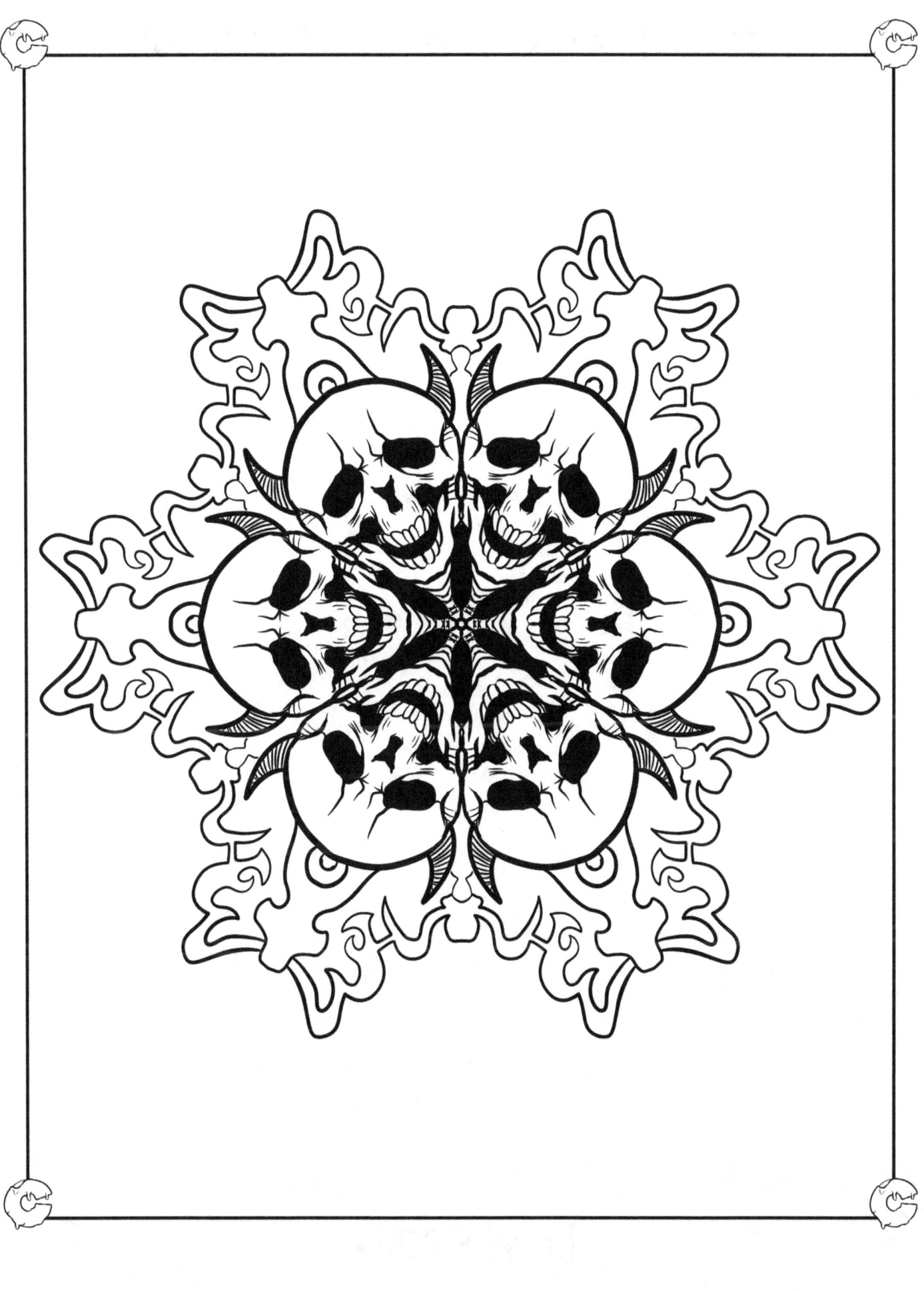

CREEPY CREATURE COLORING COLLECTION

BY JAKE PEREZ

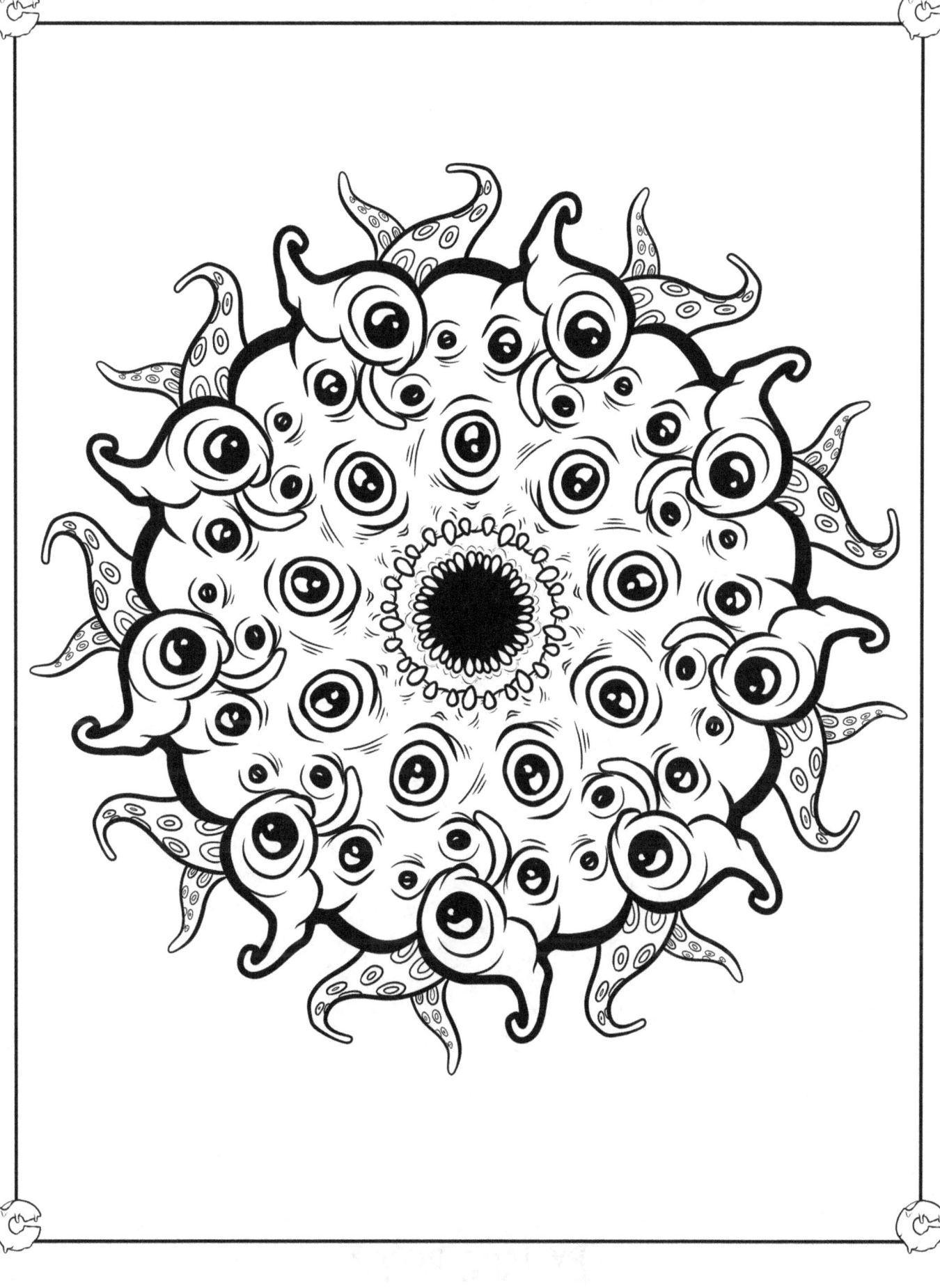

CREEPY CREATURE COLORING COLLECTION

BY JAKE PEREZ

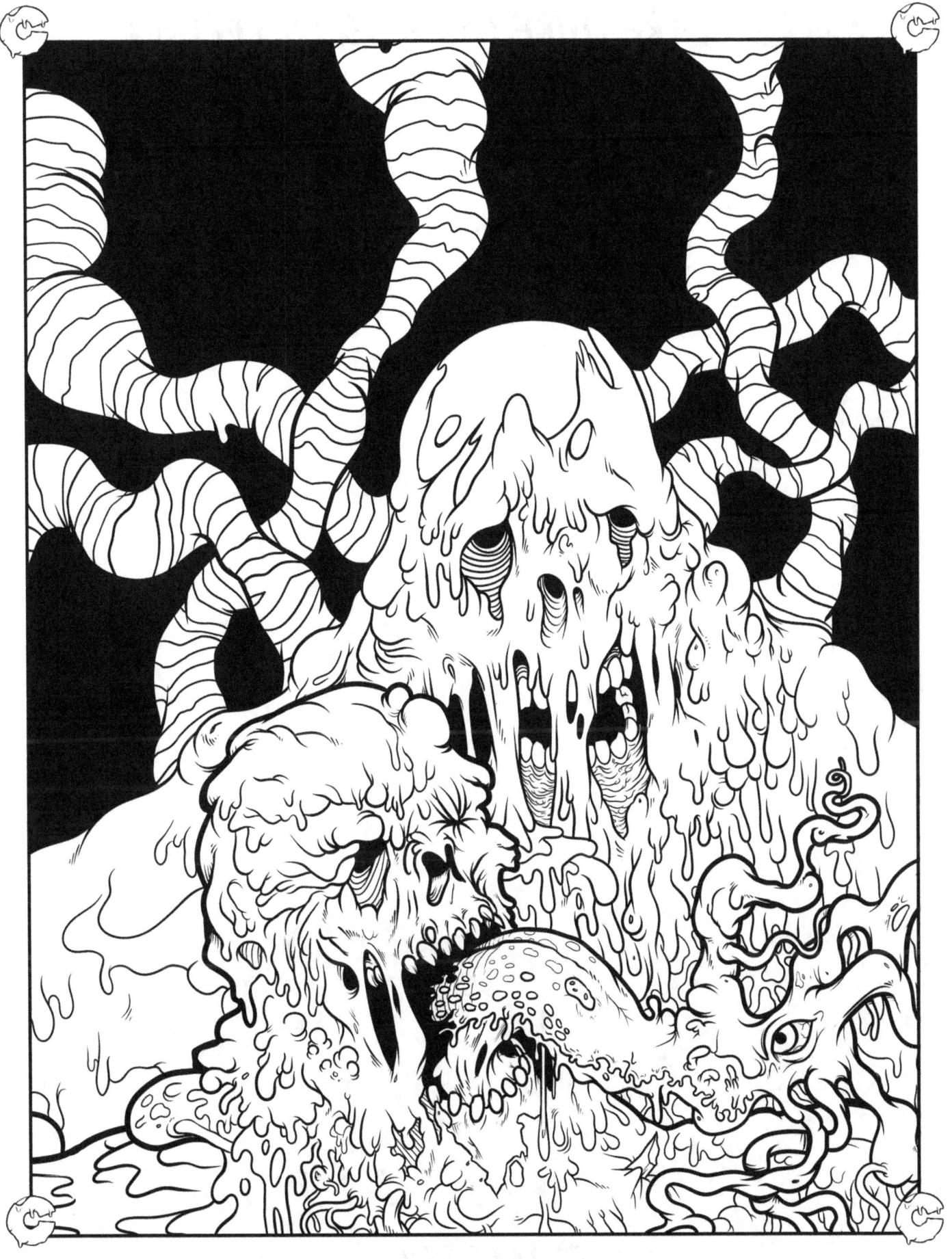

CREEPY CREATURE COLORING COLLECTION

BY JAKE PEREZ

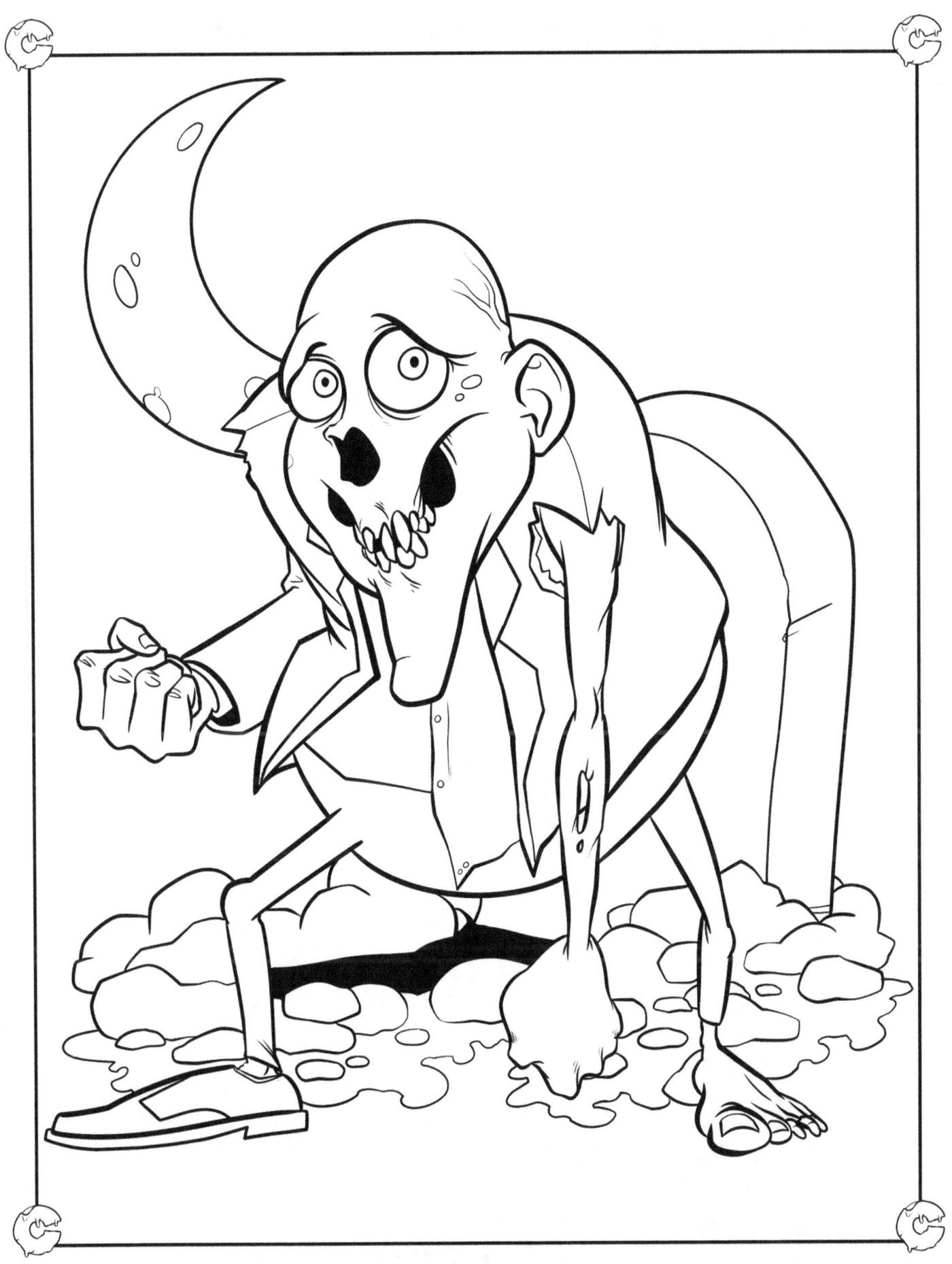

CREEPY CREATURE COLORING COLLECTION

BY JAKE PEREZ

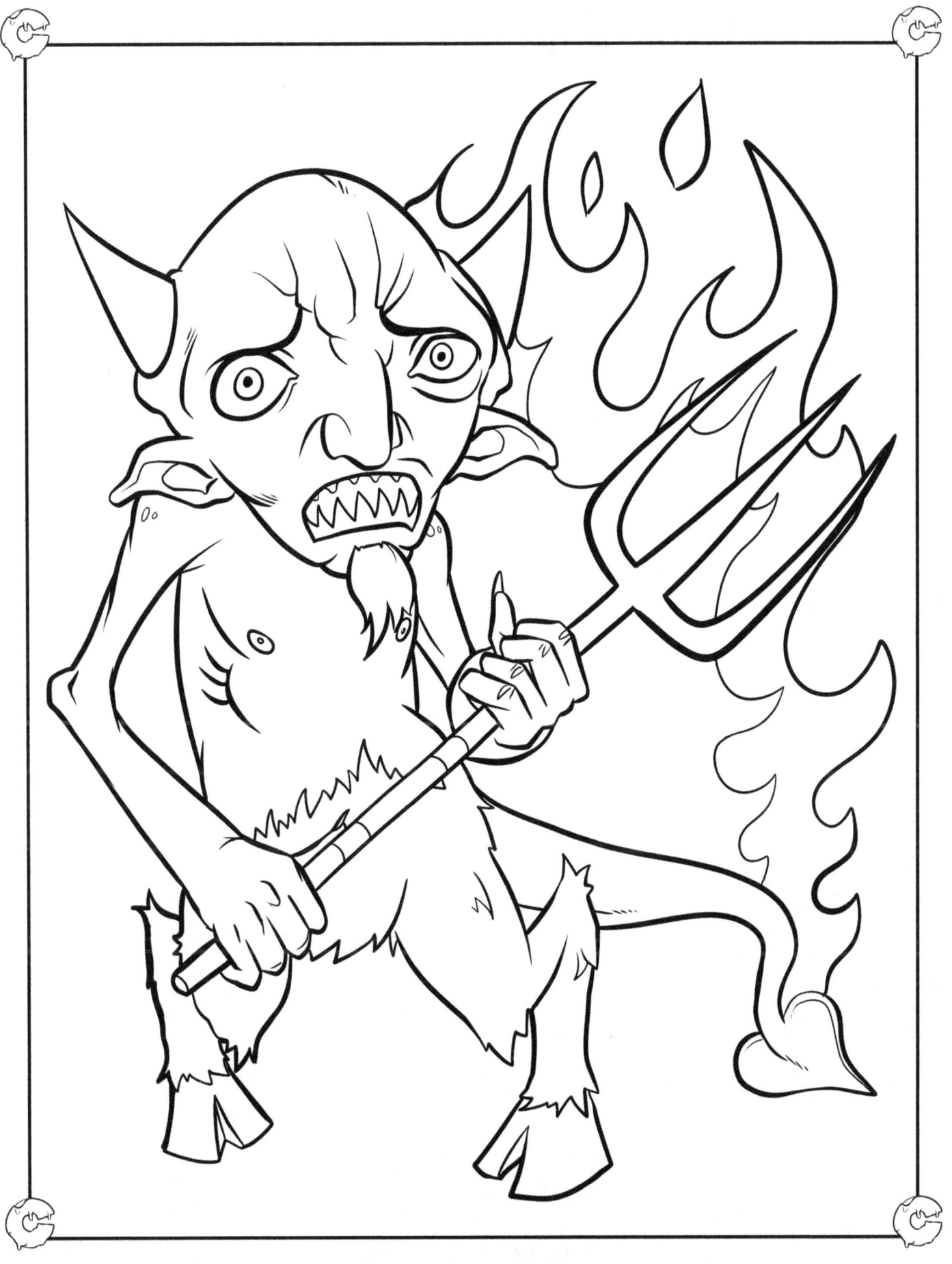

CREEPY CREATURE COLORING COLLECTION

BY JAKE PEREZ

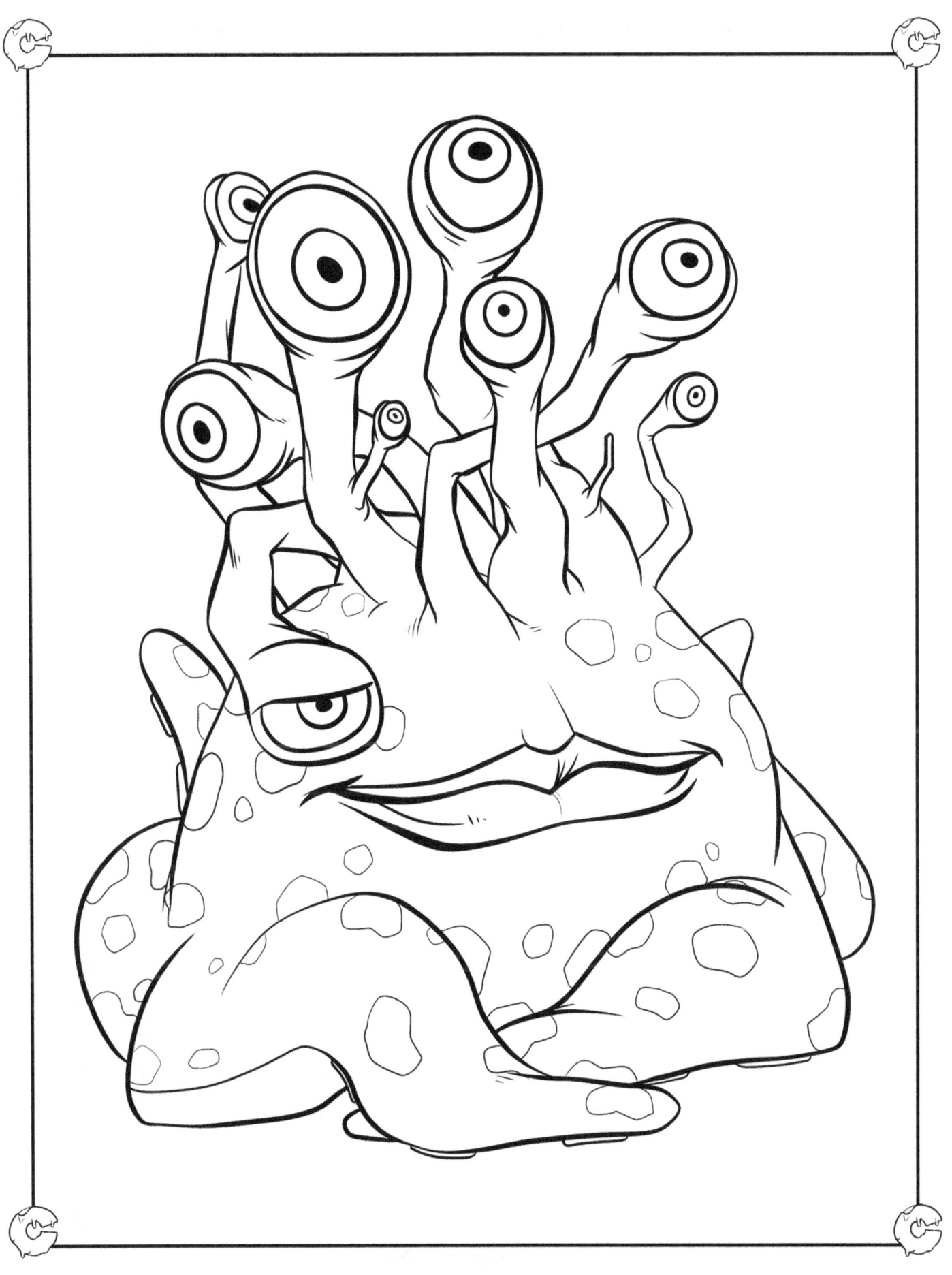

CREEPY CREATURE COLORING COLLECTION

BY JAKE PEREZ

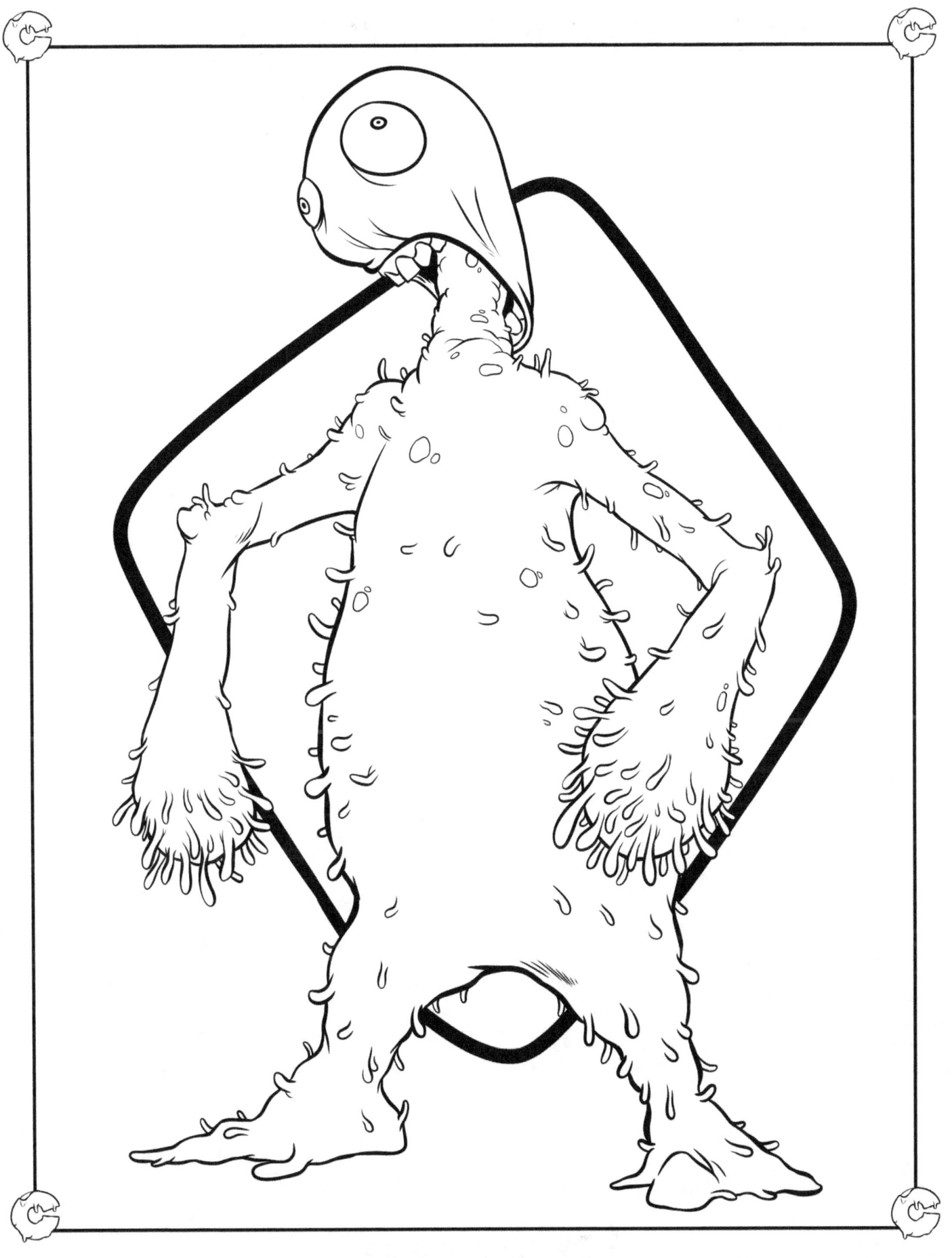

CREEPY CREATURE COLORING COLLECTION

BY JAKE PEREZ

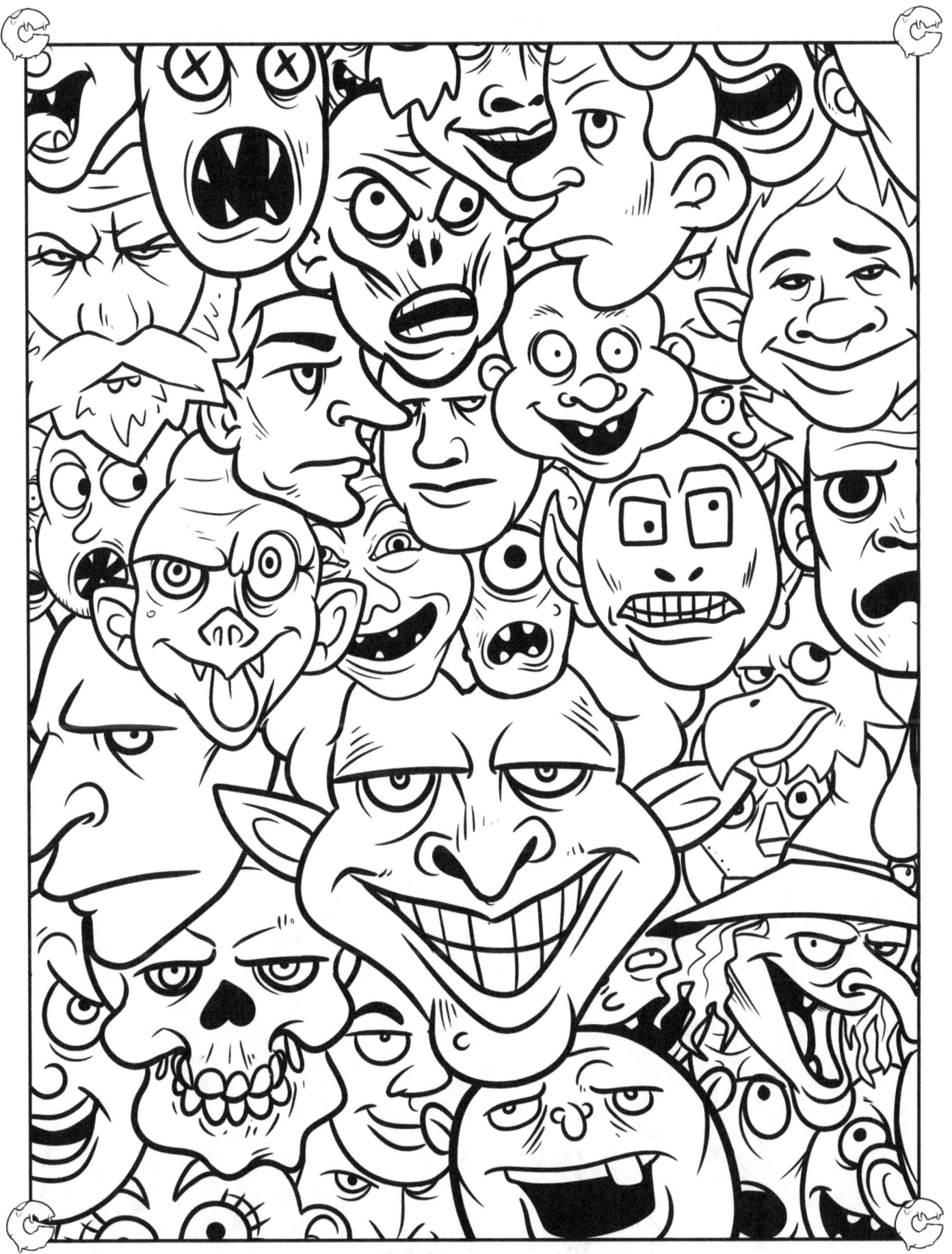

CREEPY CREATURE COLORING COLLECTION

BY JAKE PEREZ

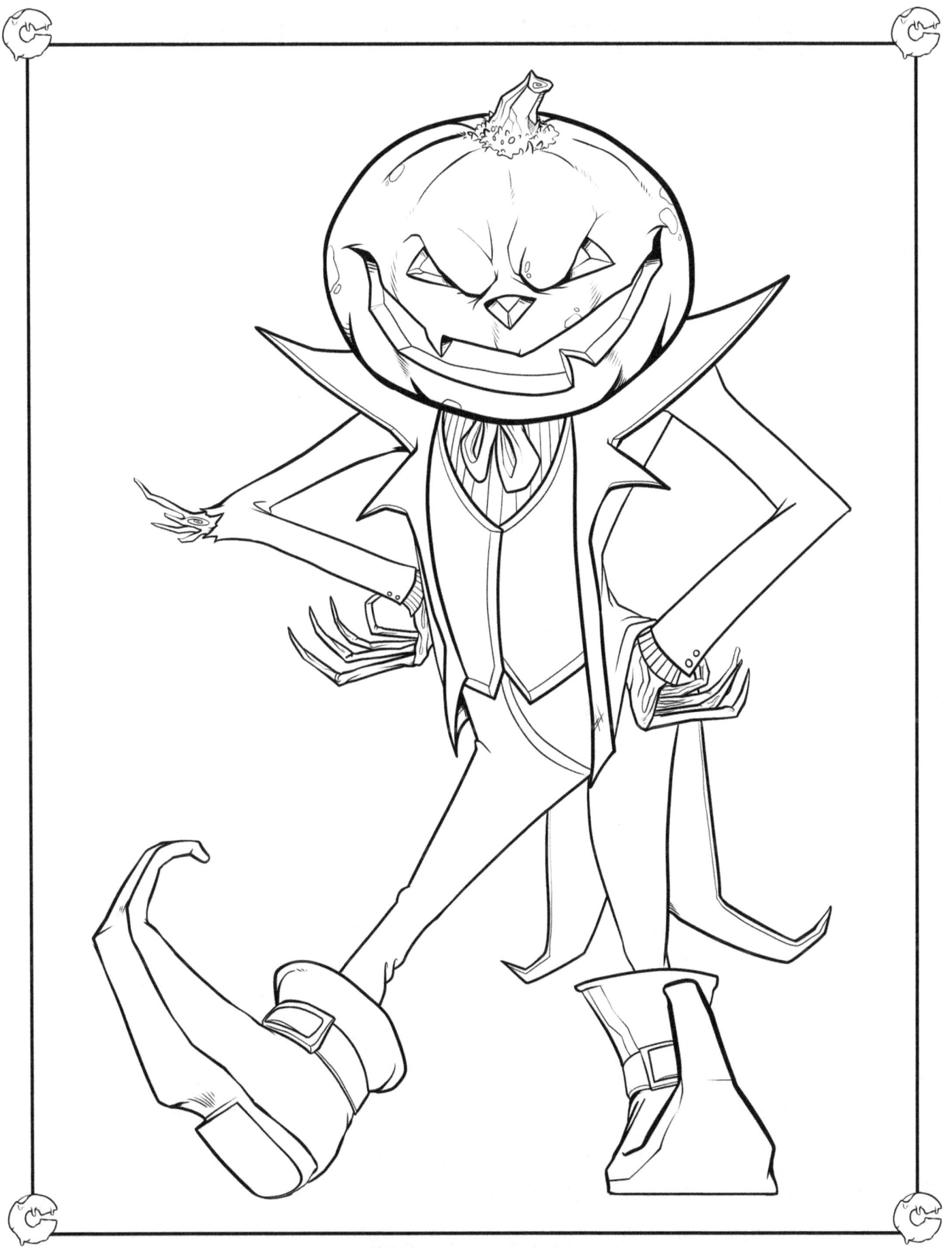

CREEPY CREATURE COLORING COLLECTION

BY JAKE PEREZ

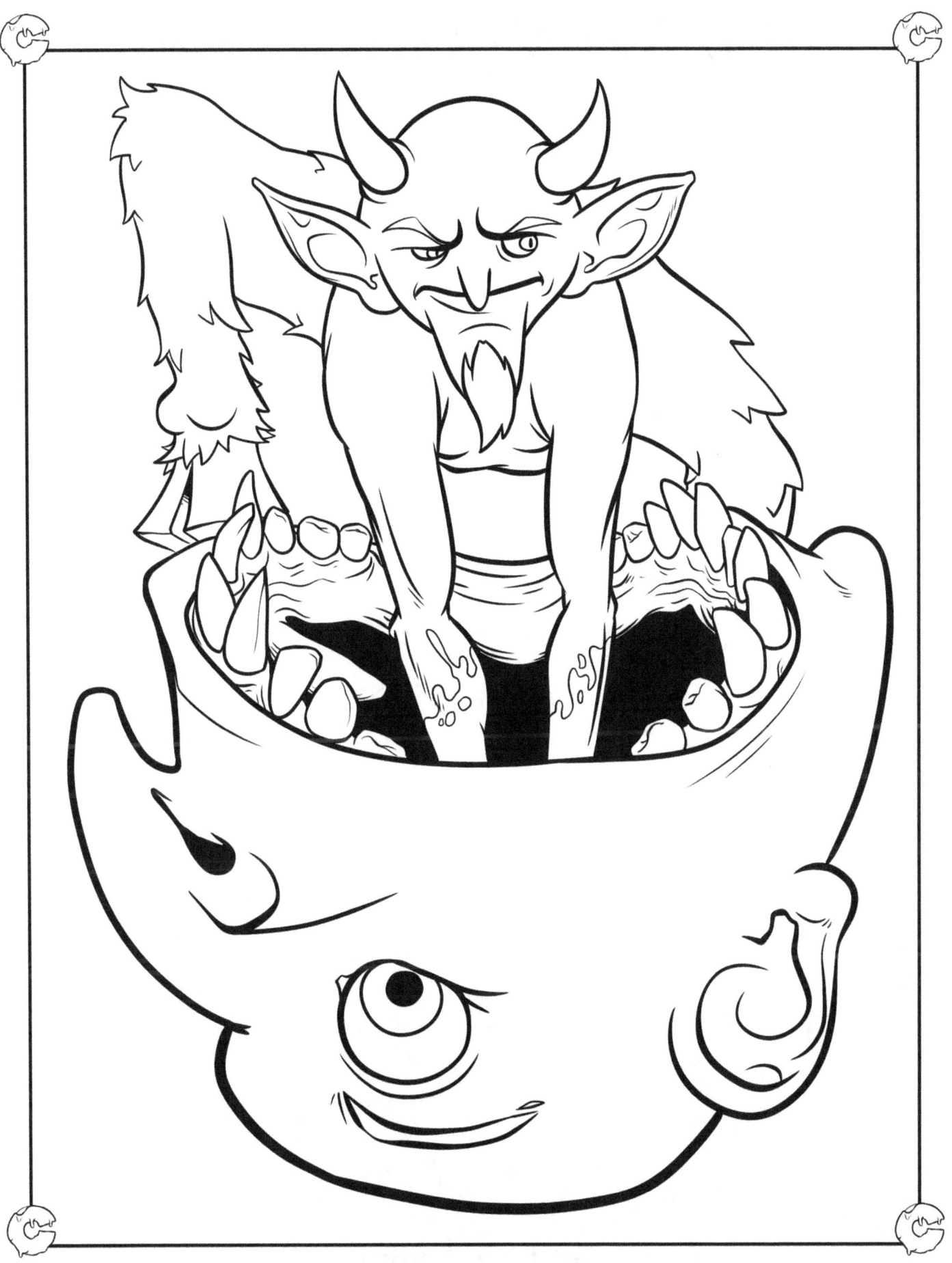

CREEPY CREATURE COLORING COLLECTION

BY JAKE PEREZ

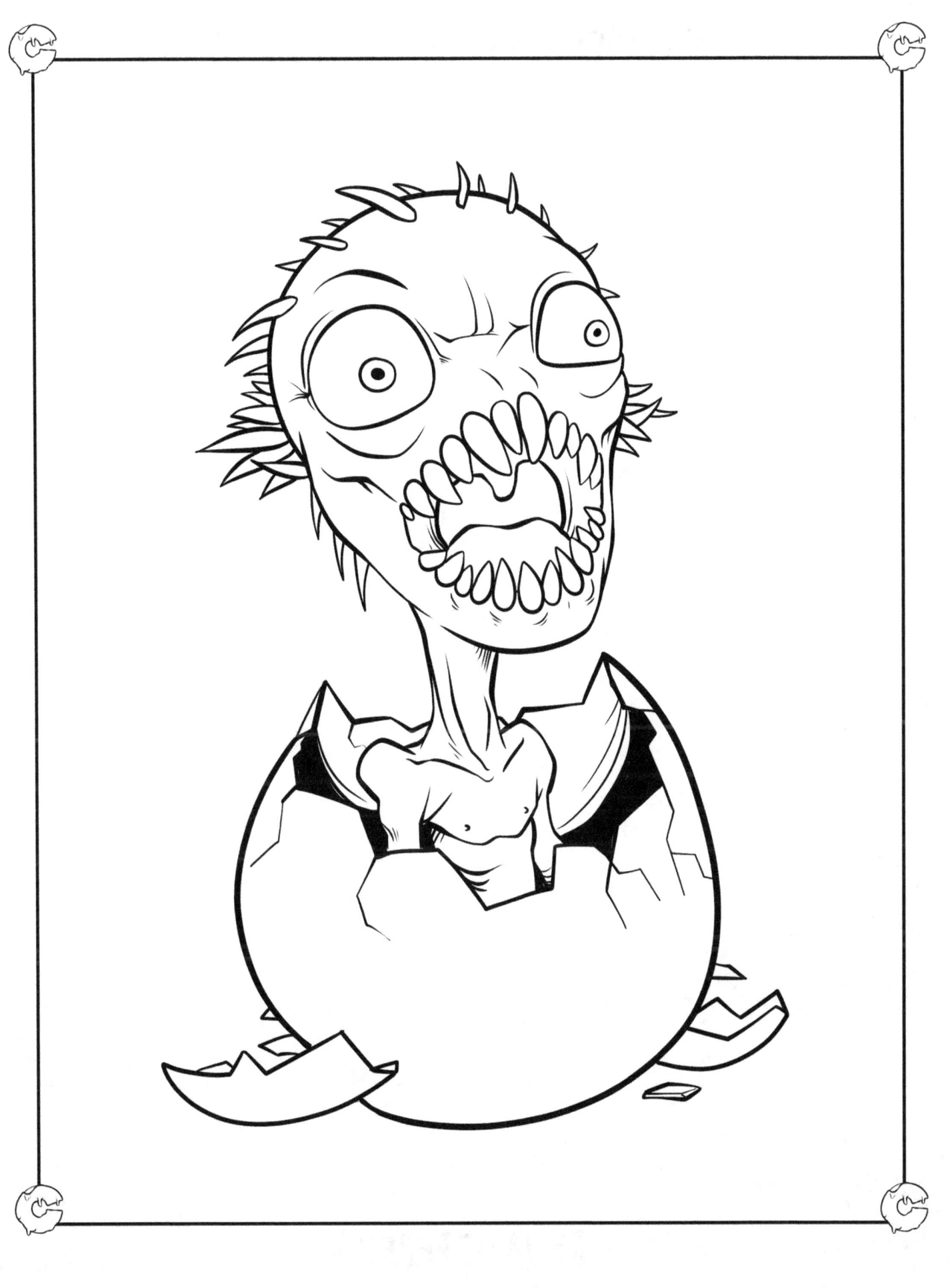

CREEPY CREATURE COLORING COLLECTION

BY JAKE PEREZ

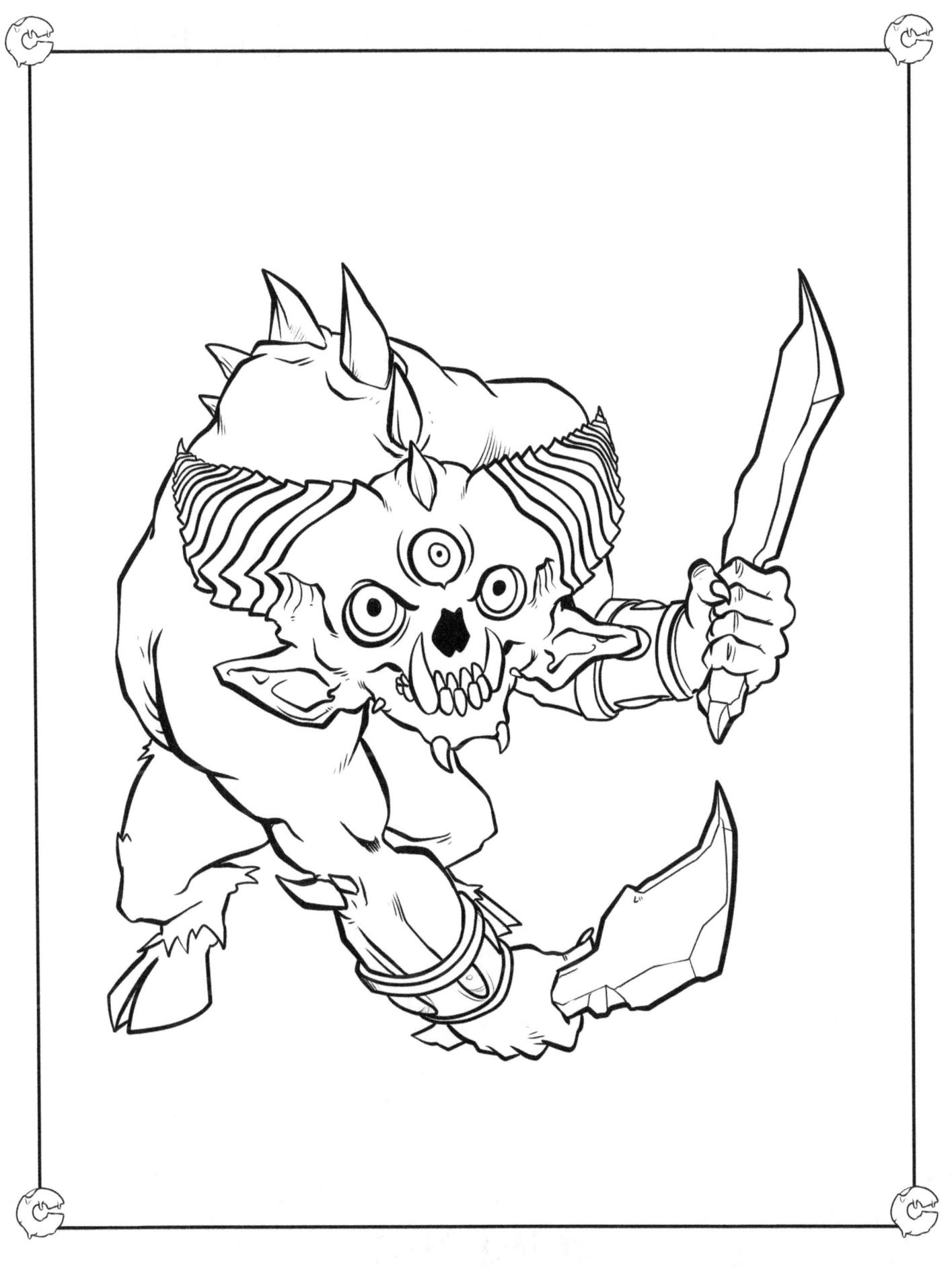

CREEPY CREATURE COLORING COLLECTION

BY JAKE PEREZ

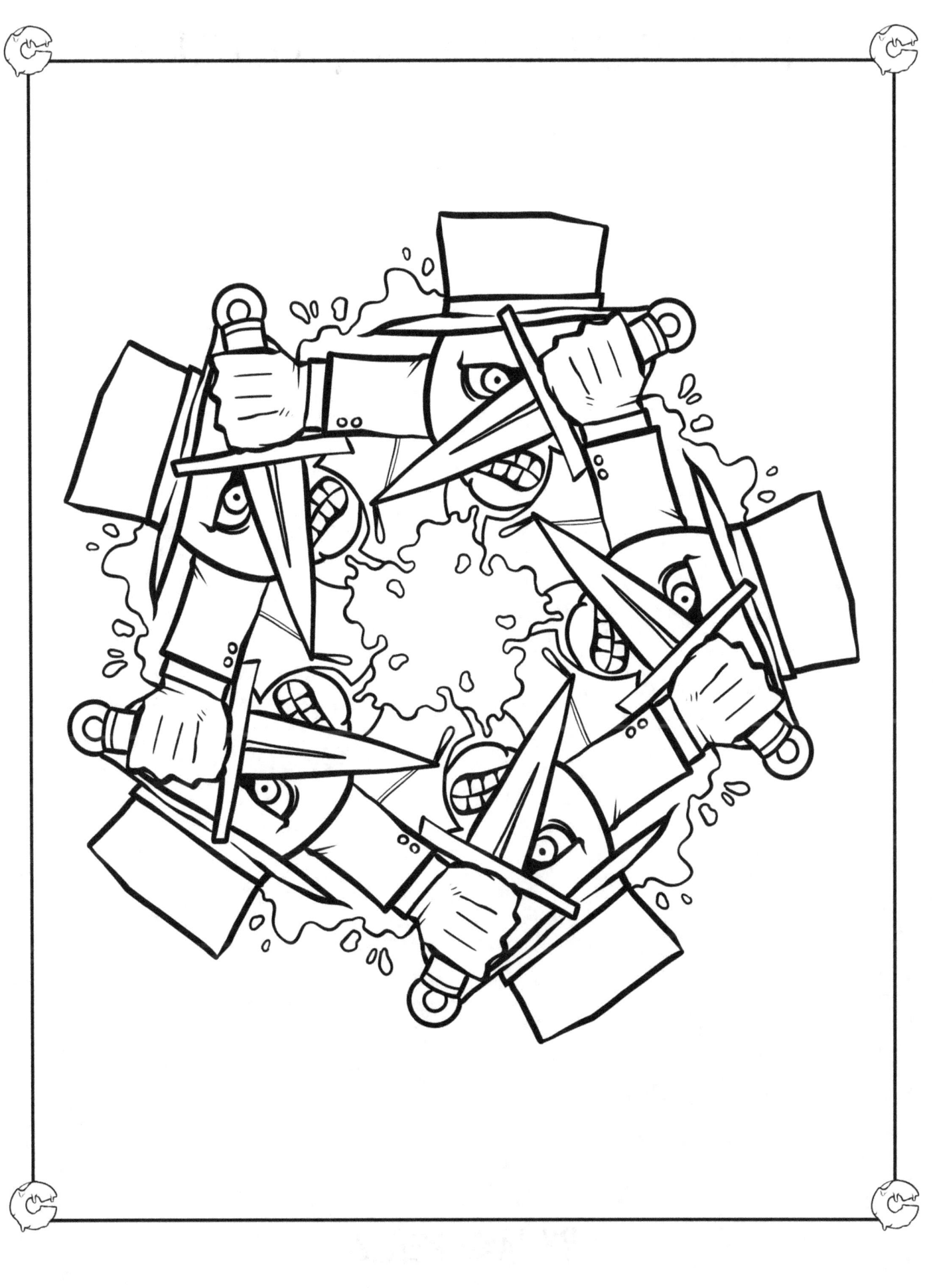

CREEPY CREATURE COLORING COLLECTION

BY JAKE PEREZ

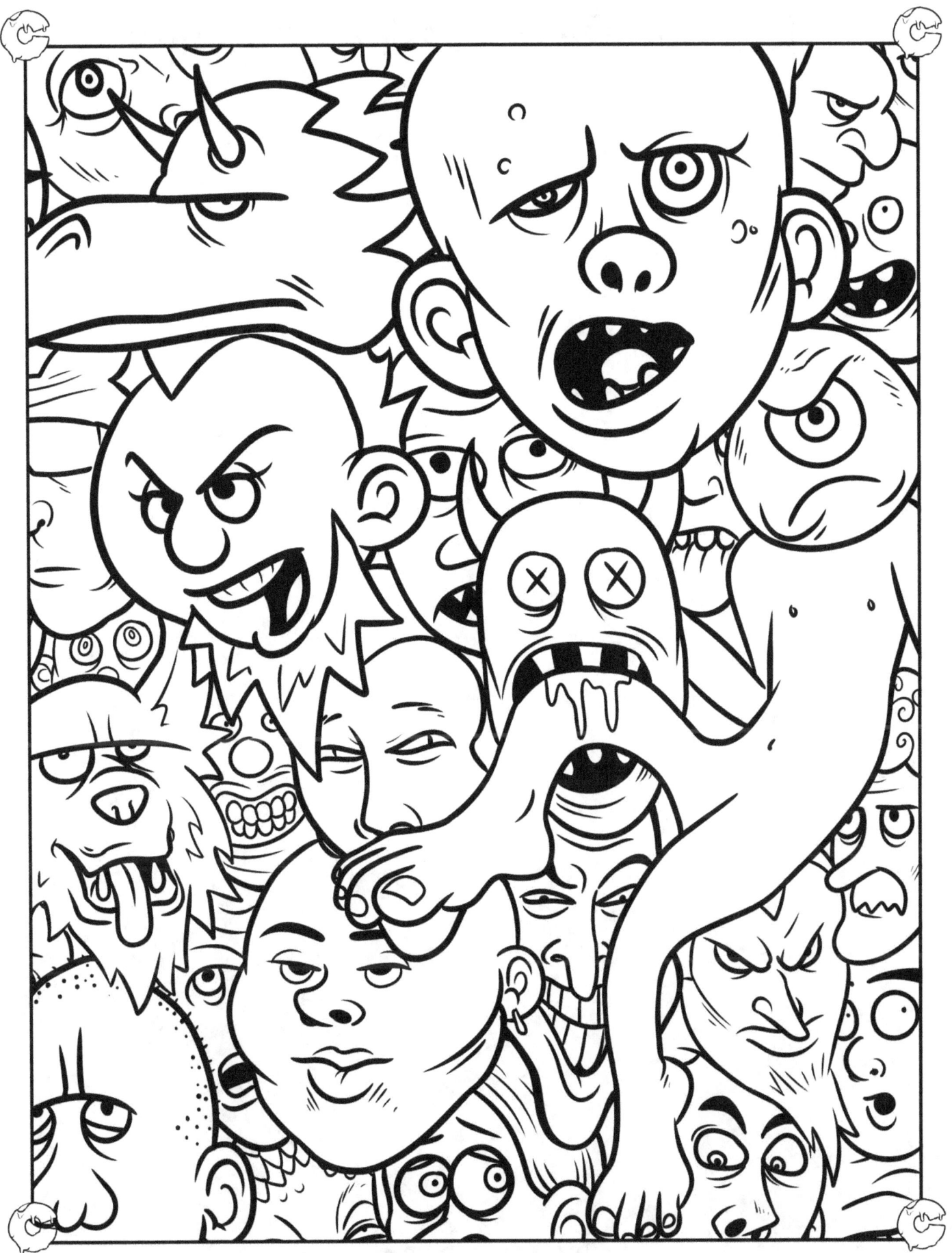

CREEPY CREATURE COLORING COLLECTION

BY JAKE PEREZ

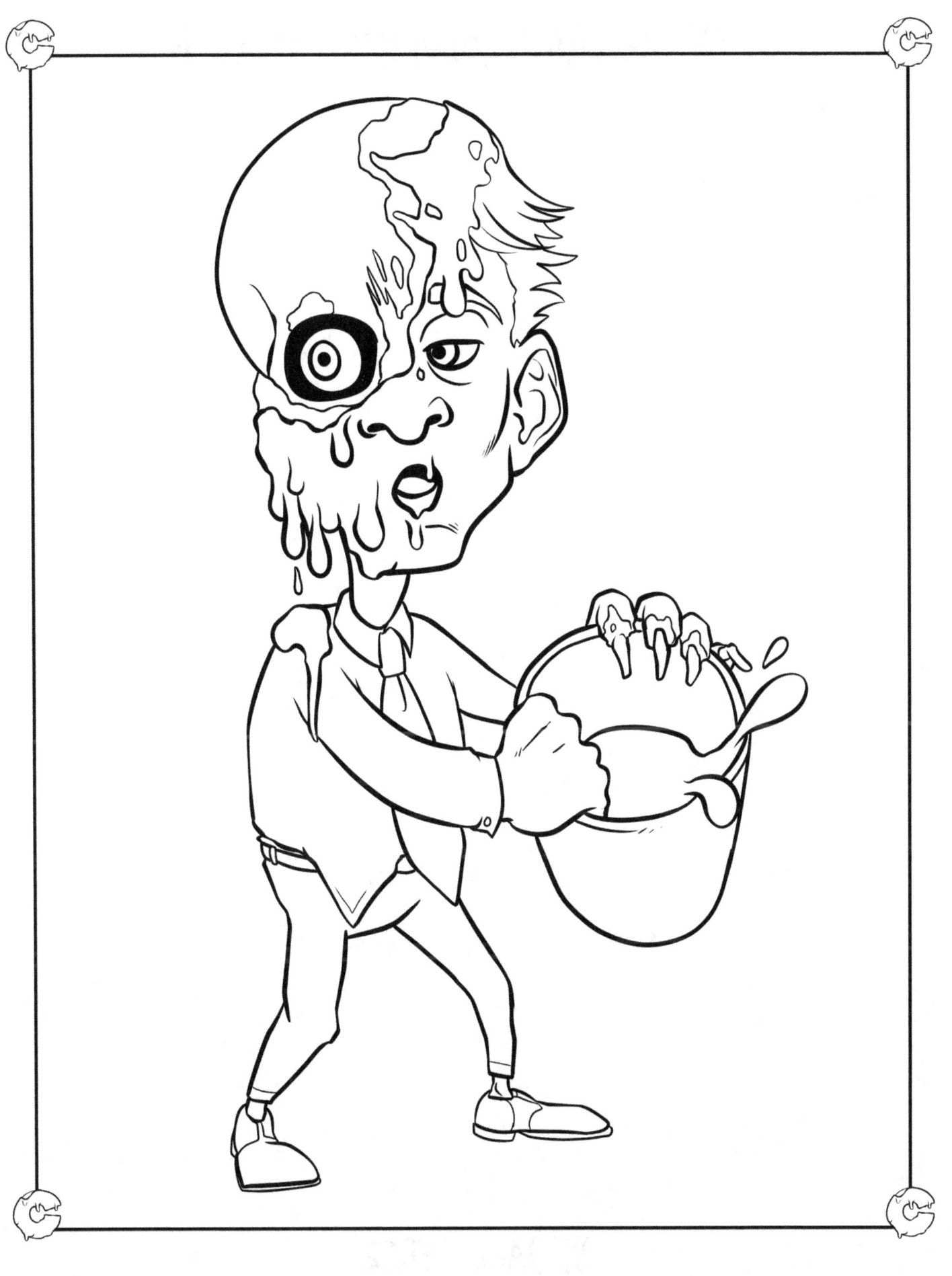

CREEPY CREATURE COLORING COLLECTION

BY JAKE PEREZ

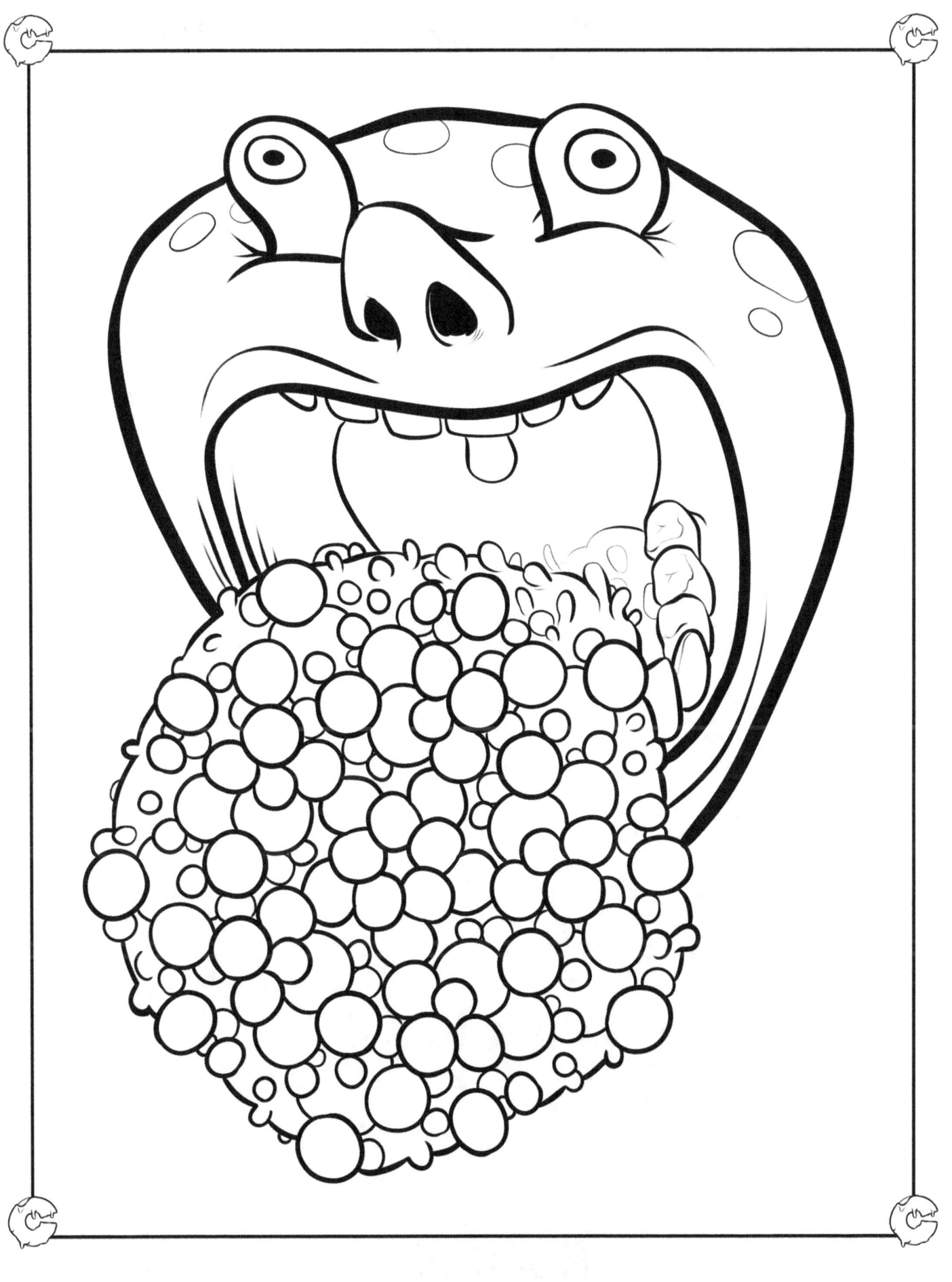

CREEPY CREATURE COLORING COLLECTION

BY JAKE PEREZ

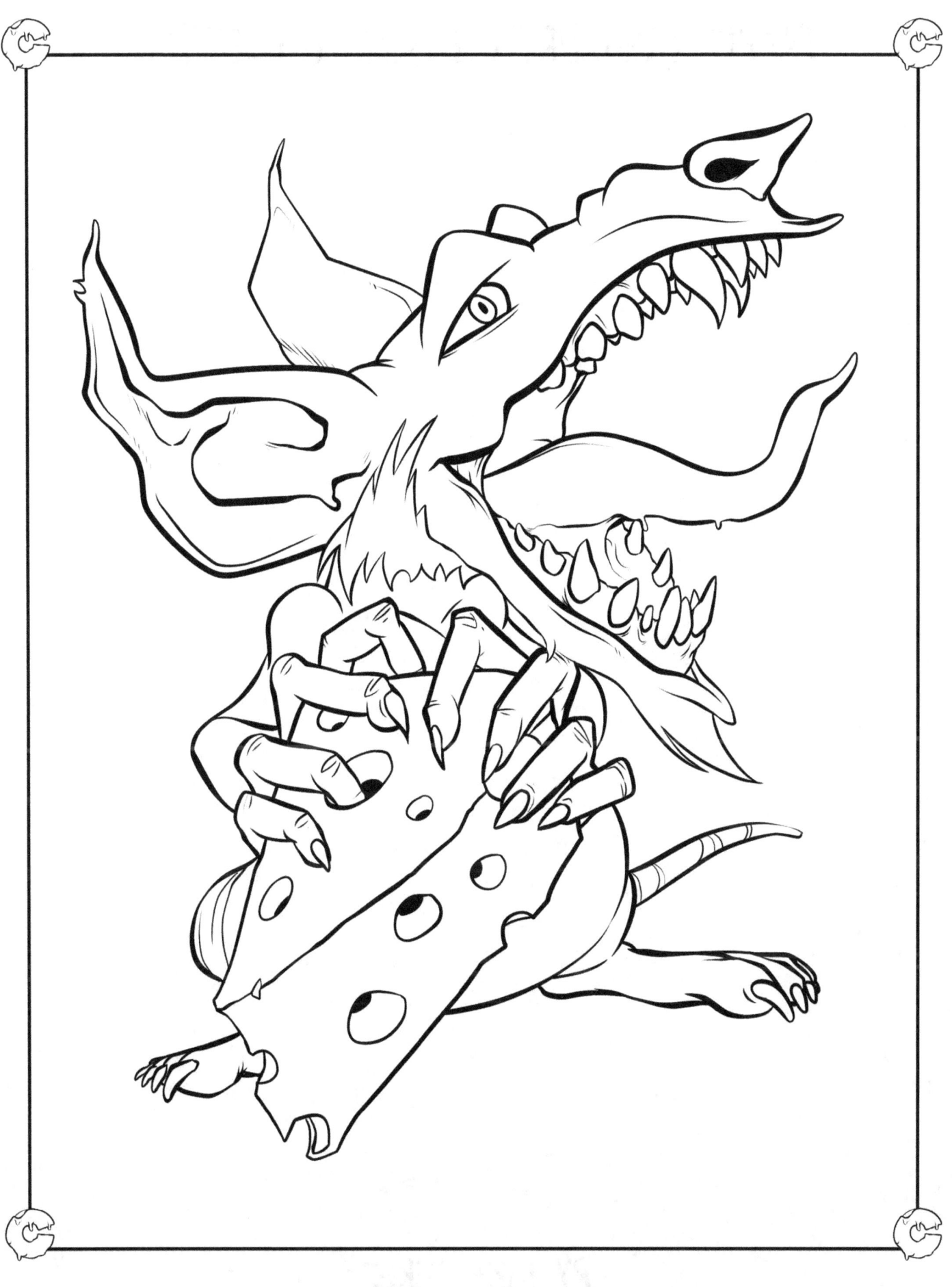

CREEPY CREATURE COLORING COLLECTION

BY JAKE PEREZ

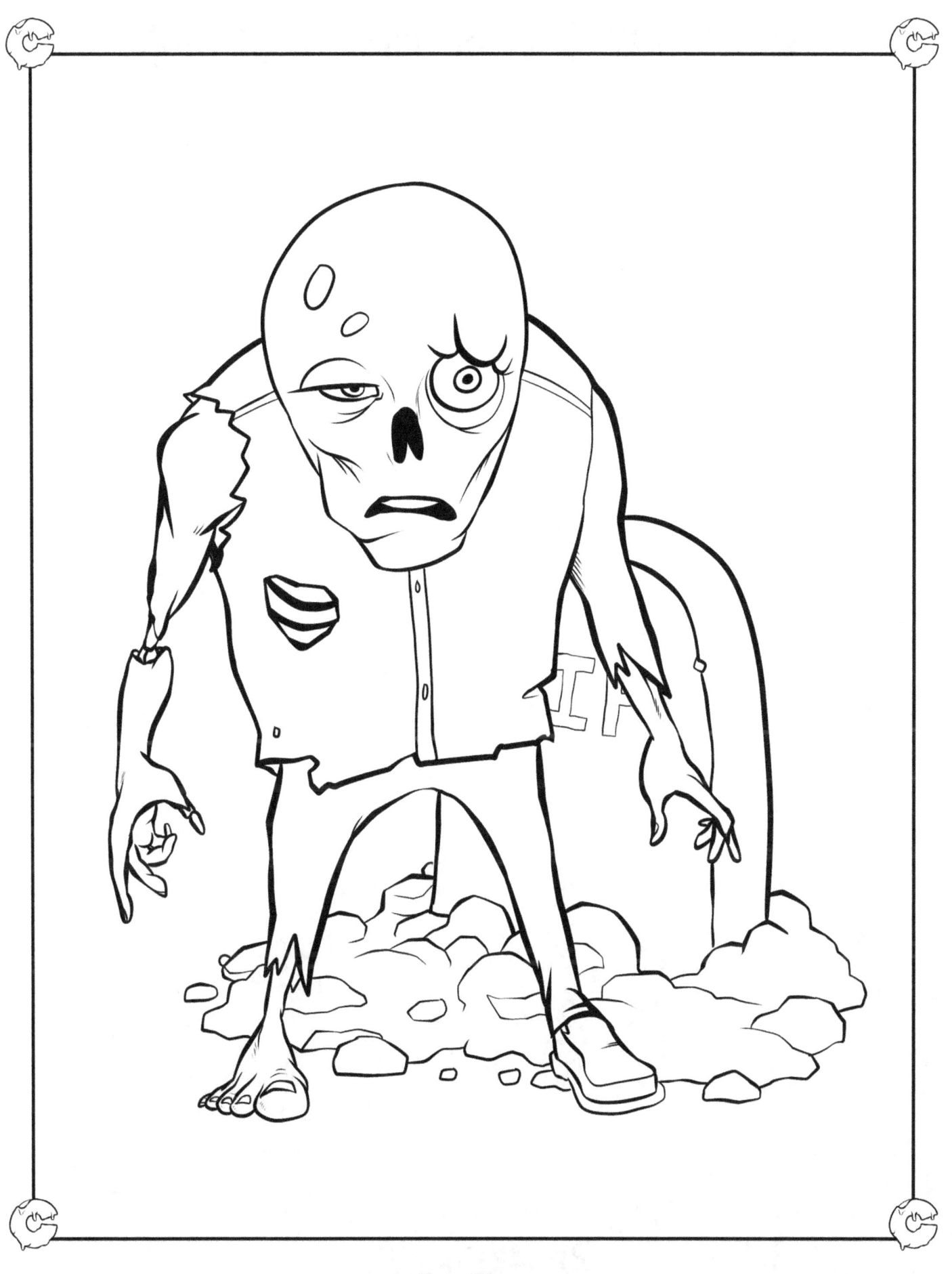

CREEPY CREATURE COLORING COLLECTION

BY JAKE PEREZ

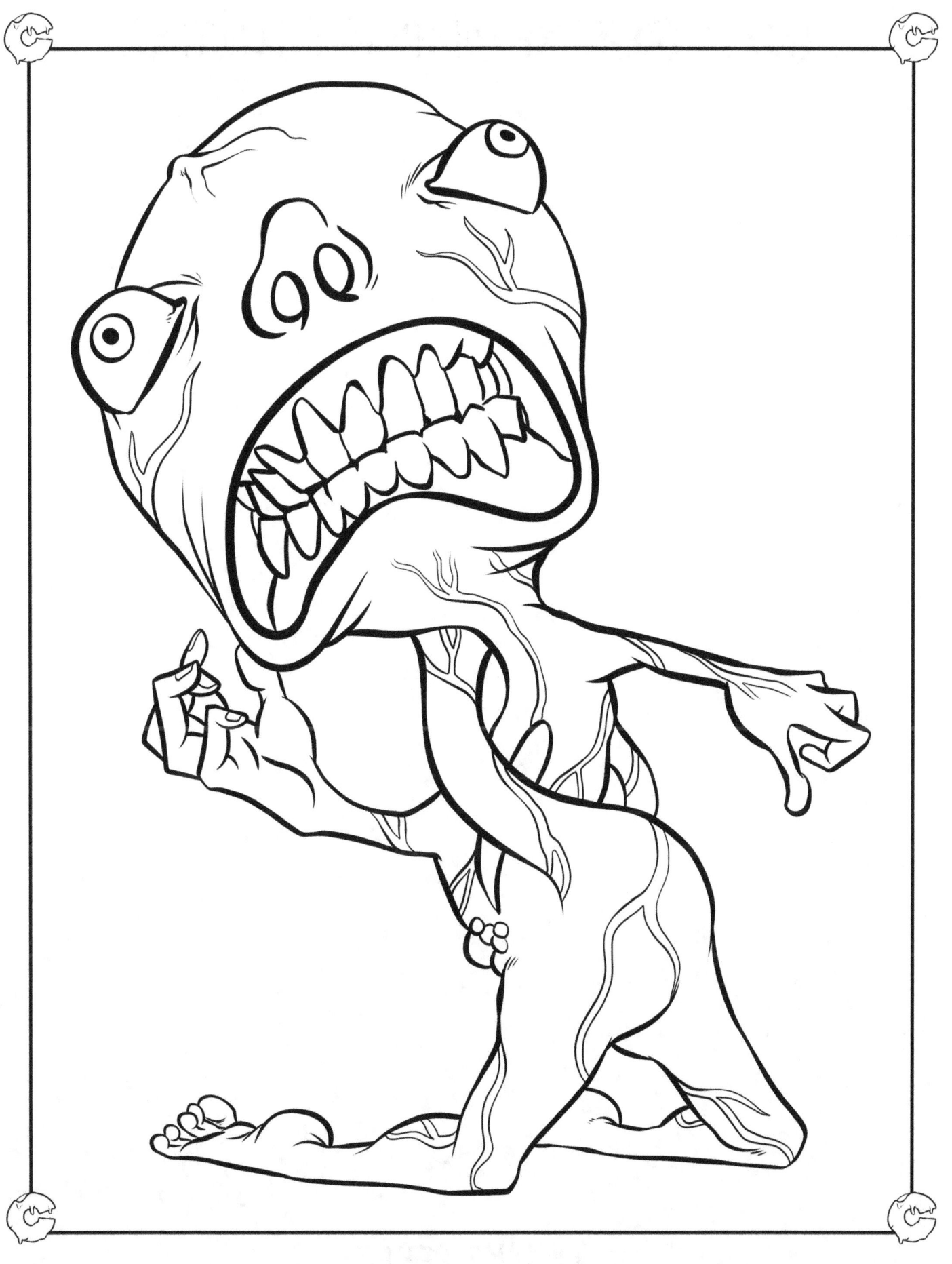

CREEPY CREATURE COLORING COLLECTION

BY JAKE PEREZ

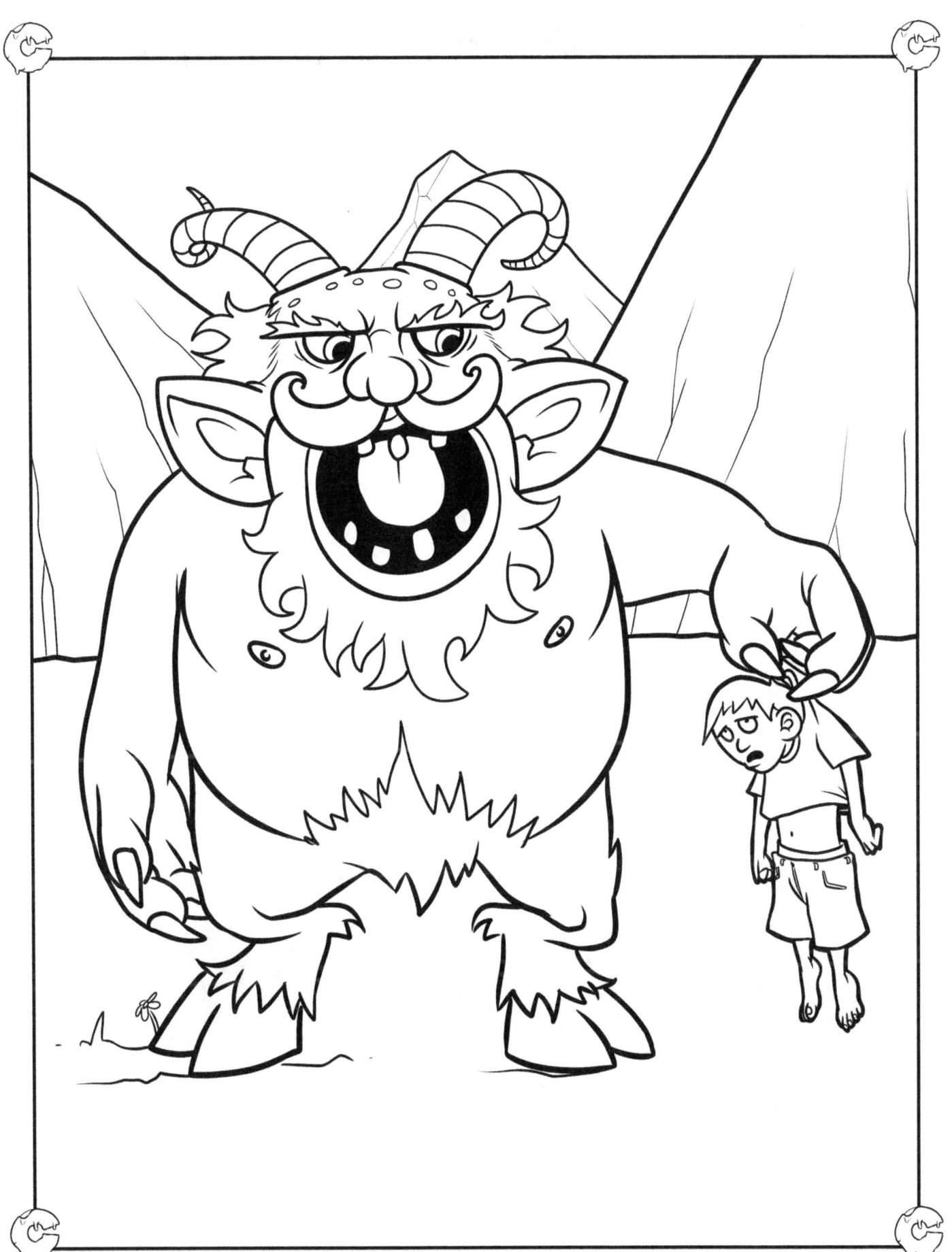

CREEPY CREATURE COLORING COLLECTION

BY JAKE PEREZ

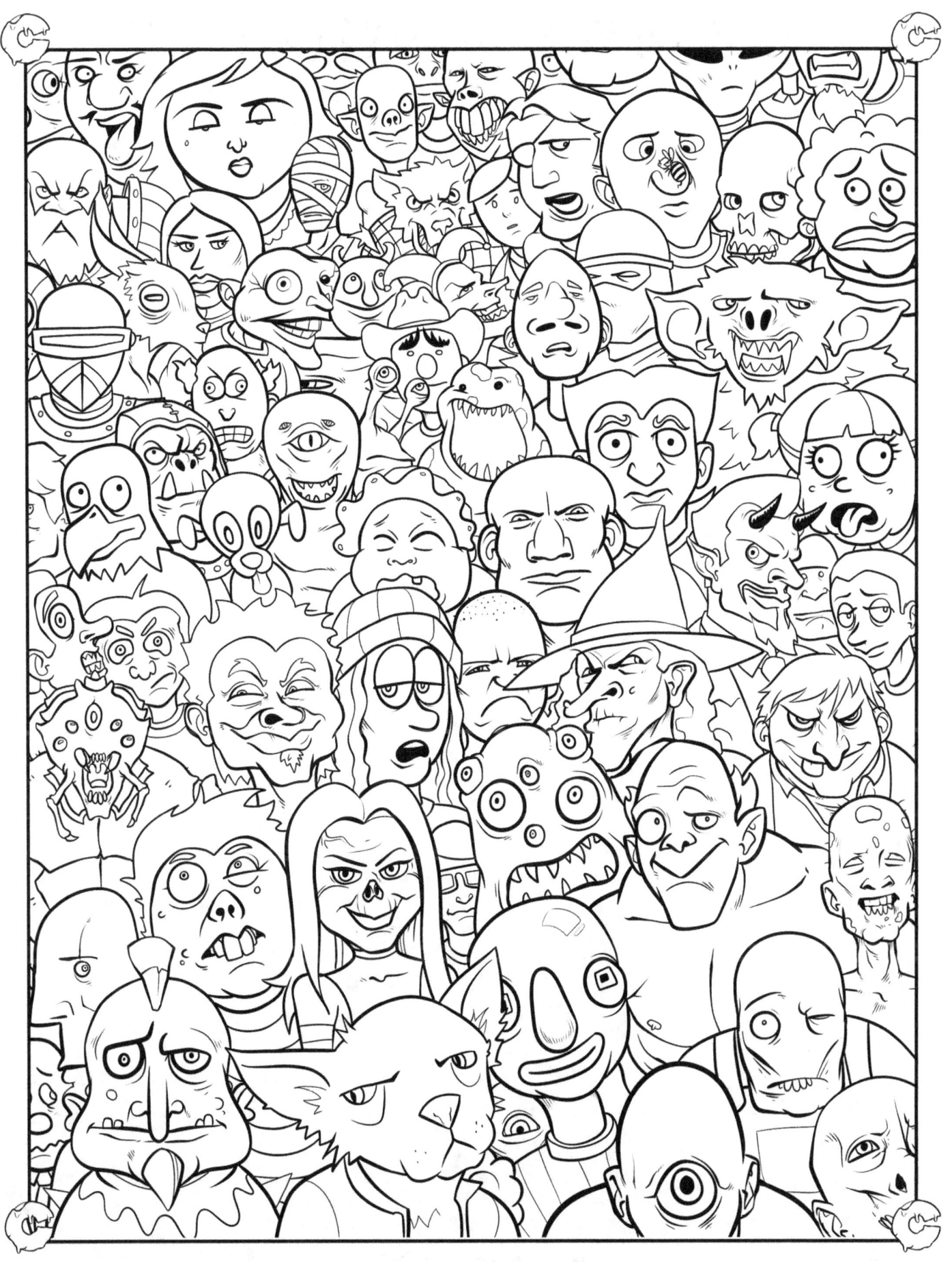

CREEPY CREATURE COLORING COLLECTION

BY JAKE PEREZ

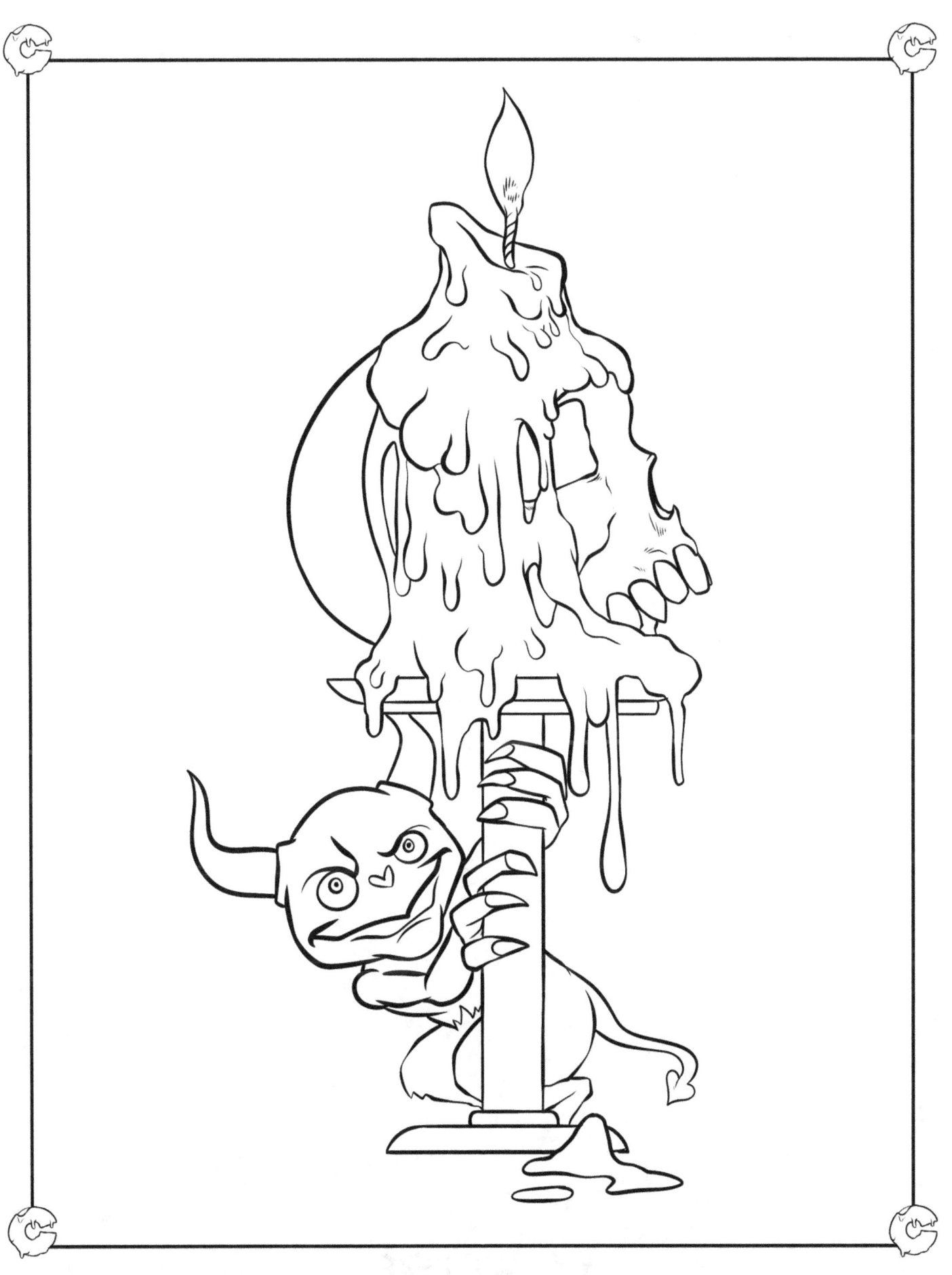

CREEPY CREATURE COLORING COLLECTION

BY JAKE PEREZ

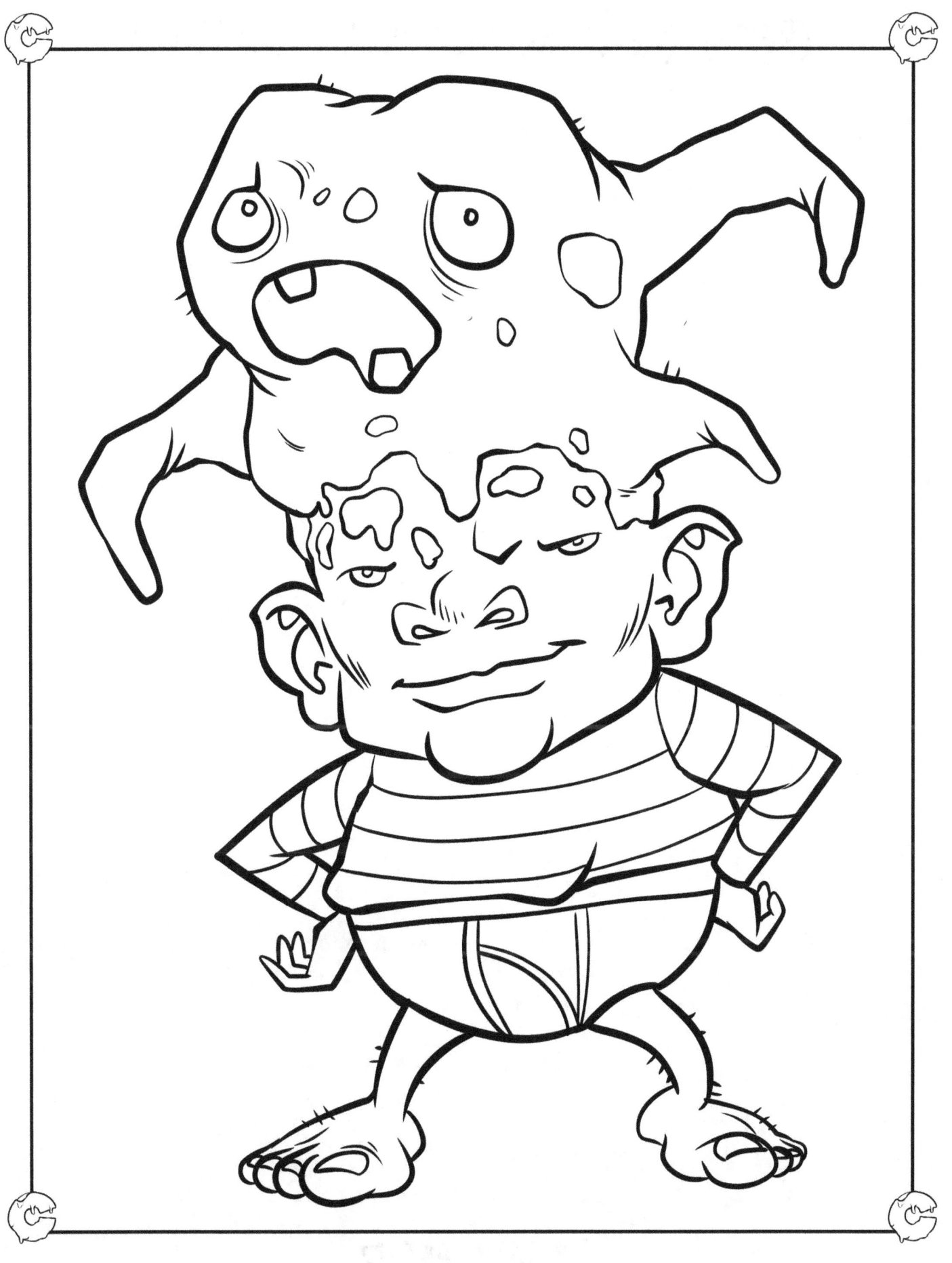

CREEPY CREATURE COLORING COLLECTION

BY JAKE PEREZ

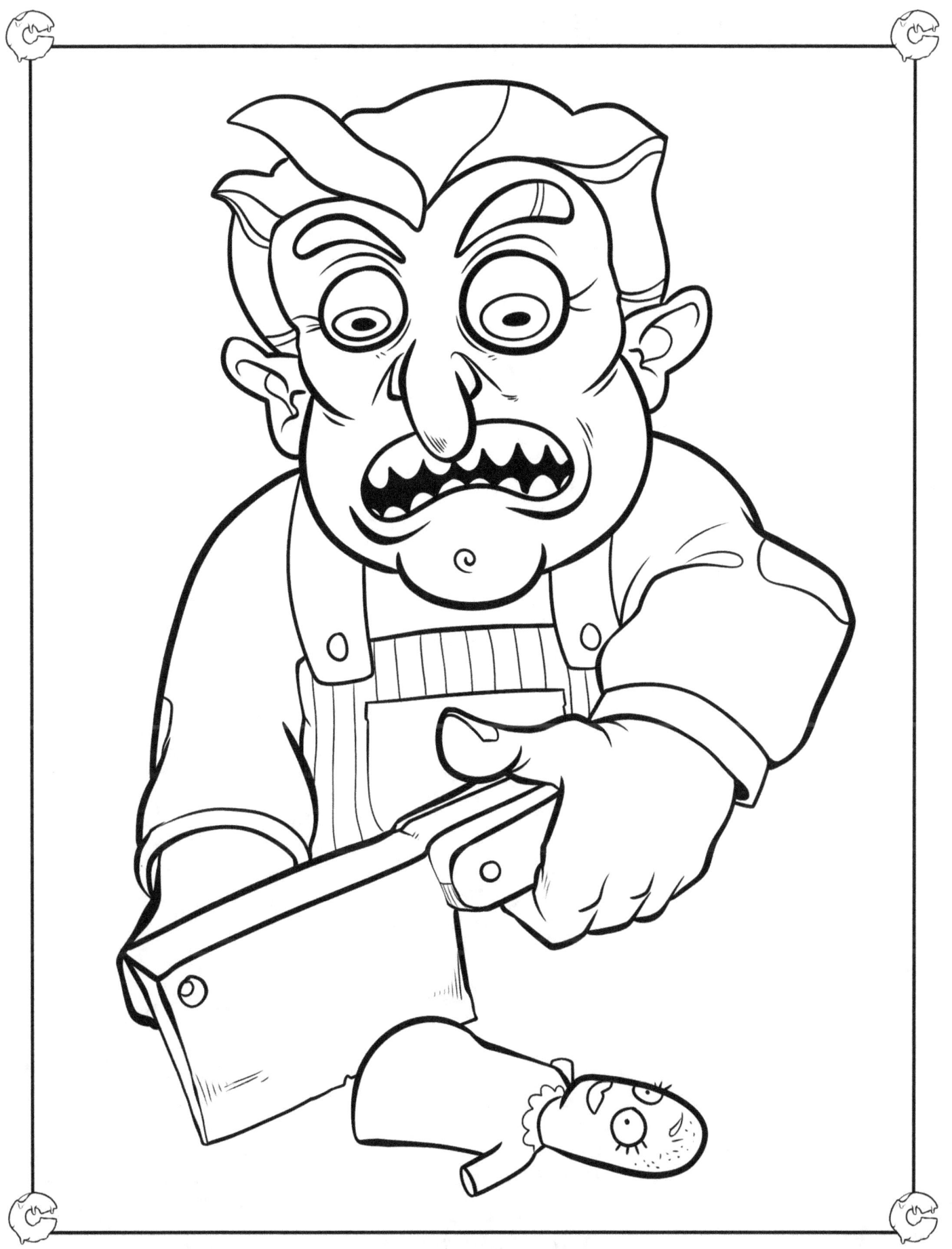

CREEPY CREATURE COLORING COLLECTION

BY JAKE PEREZ

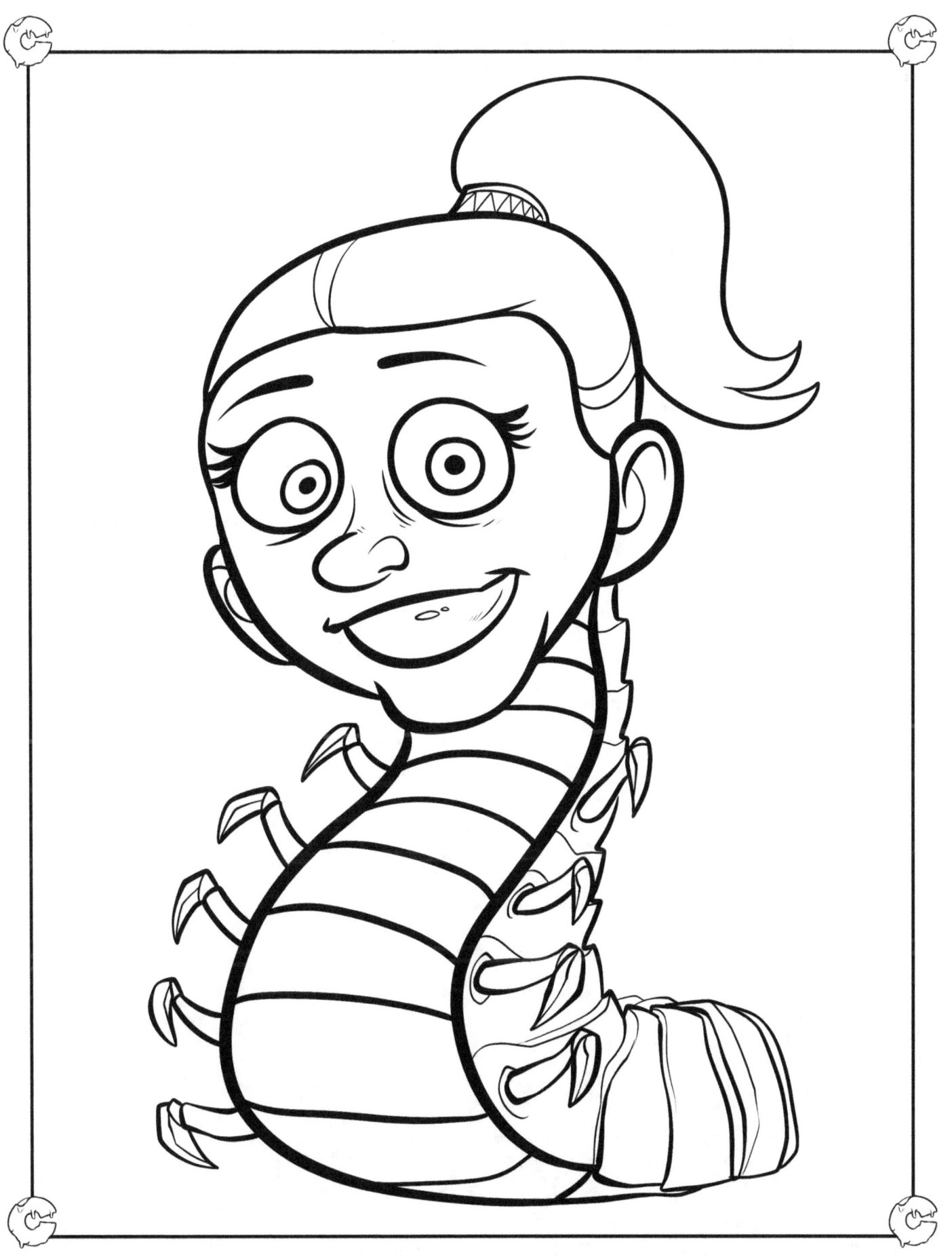

CREEPY CREATURE COLORING COLLECTION

BY JAKE PEREZ

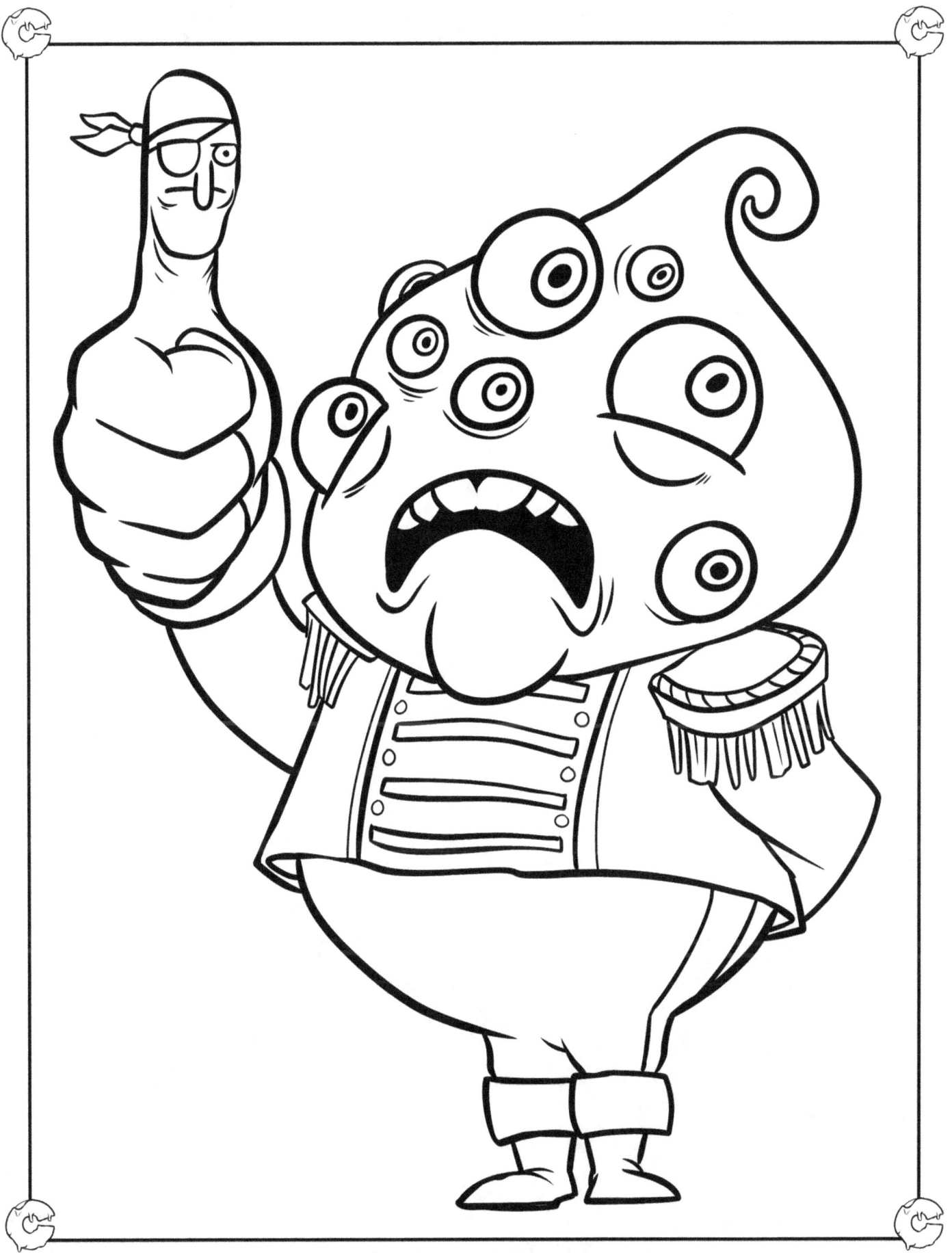

CREEPY CREATURE COLORING COLLECTION

BY JAKE PEREZ

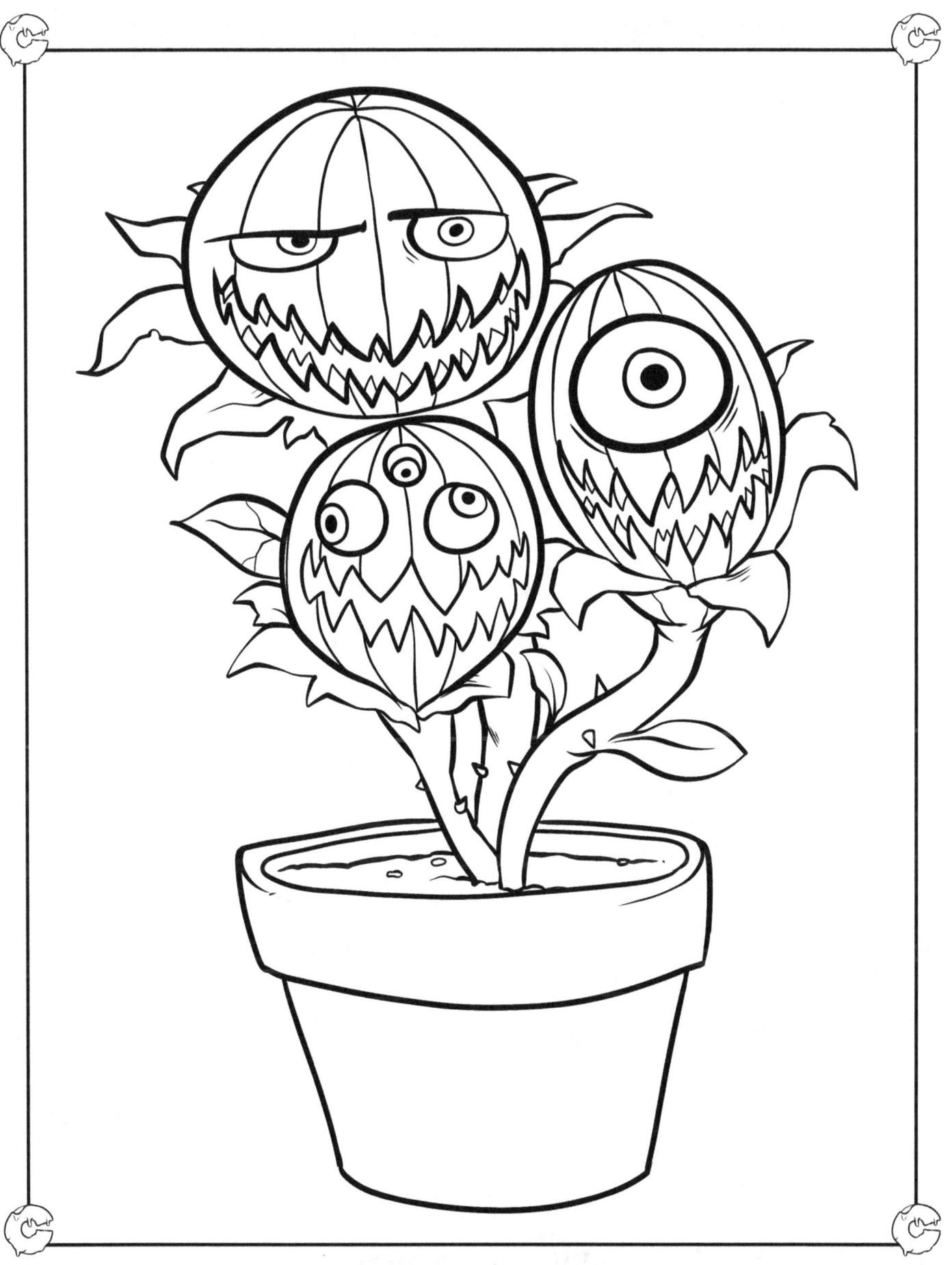

CREEPY CREATURE COLORING COLLECTION

BY JAKE PEREZ

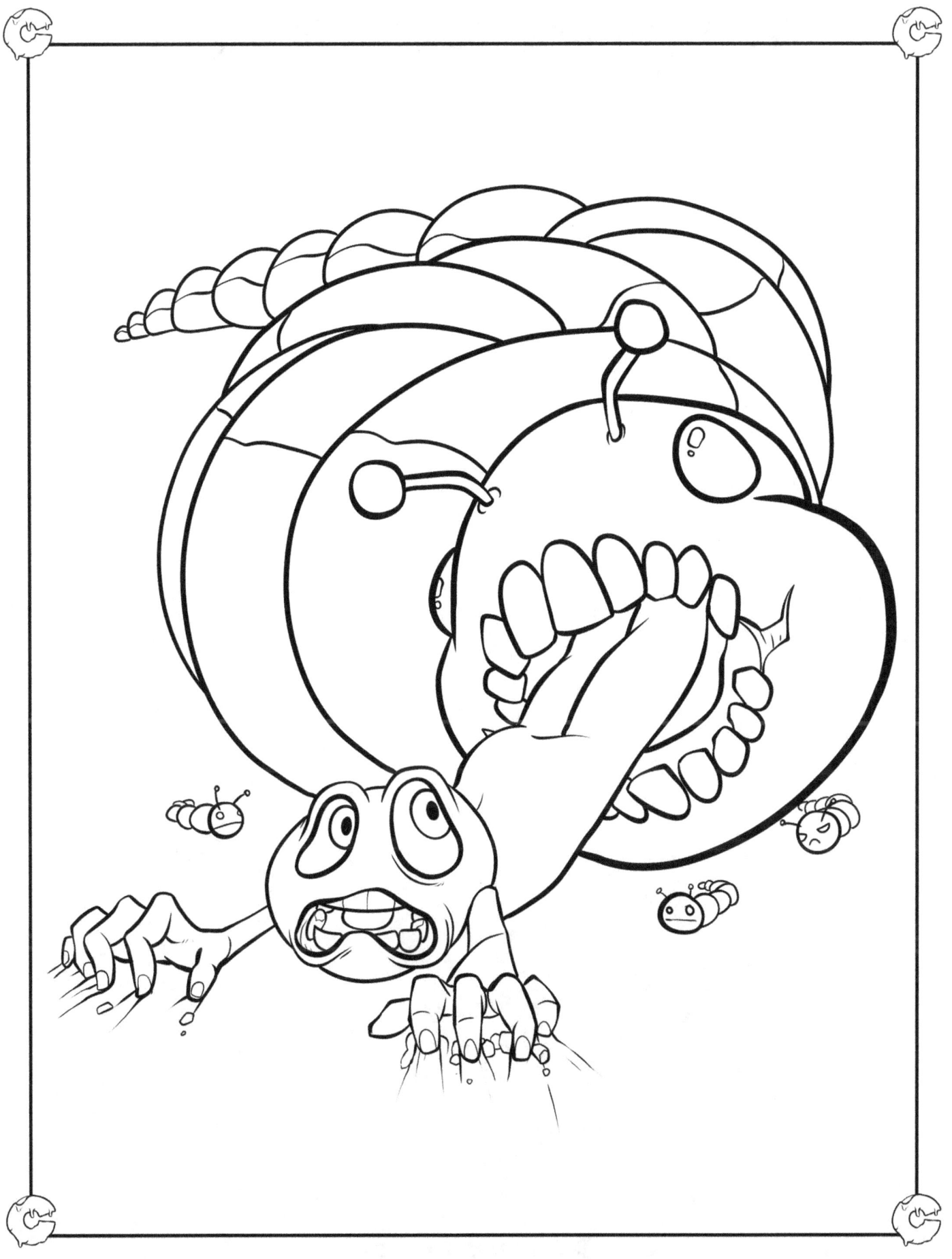

CREEPY CREATURE COLORING COLLECTION

BY JAKE PEREZ

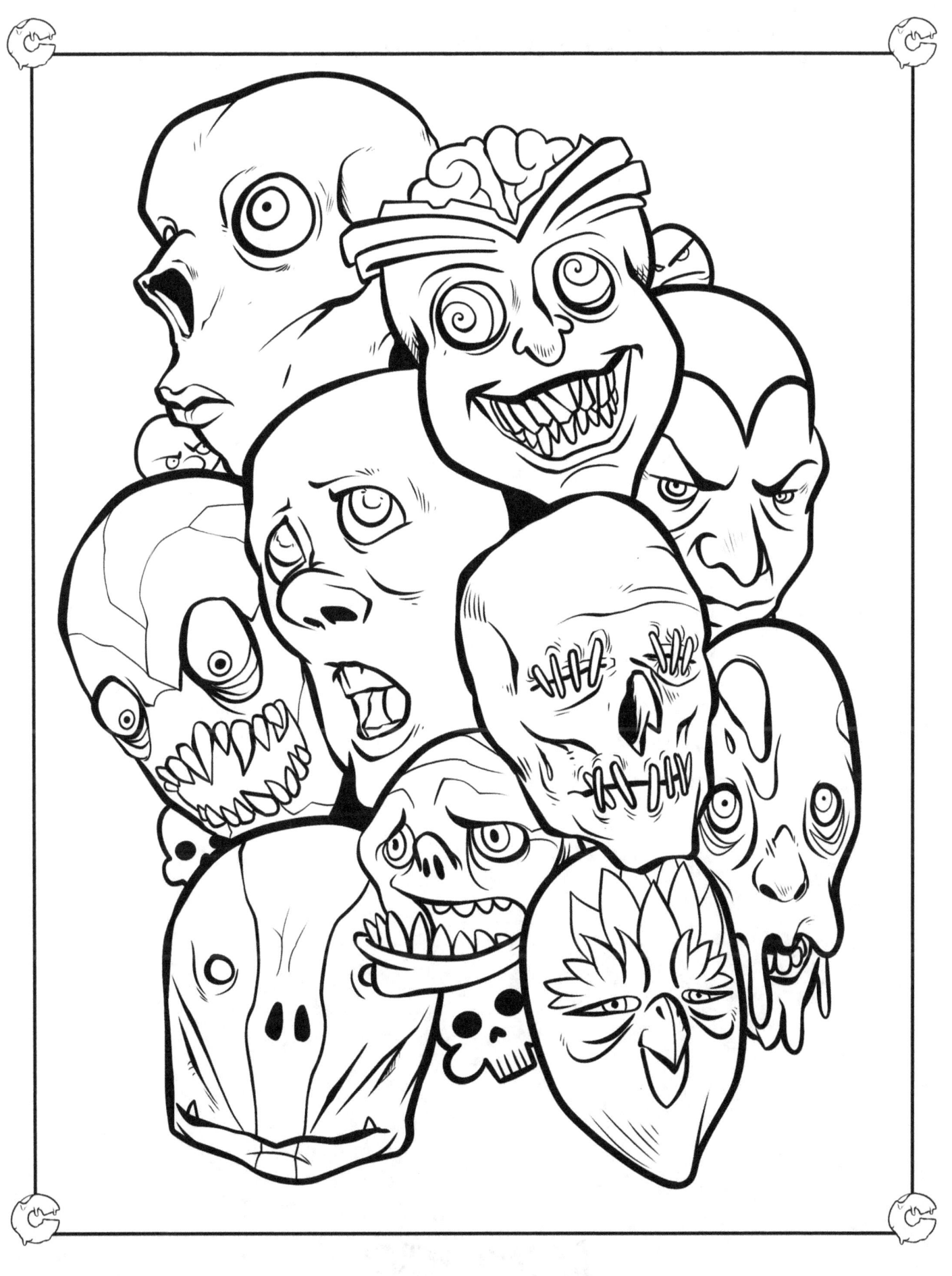

CREEPY CREATURE COLORING COLLECTION

BY JAKE PEREZ

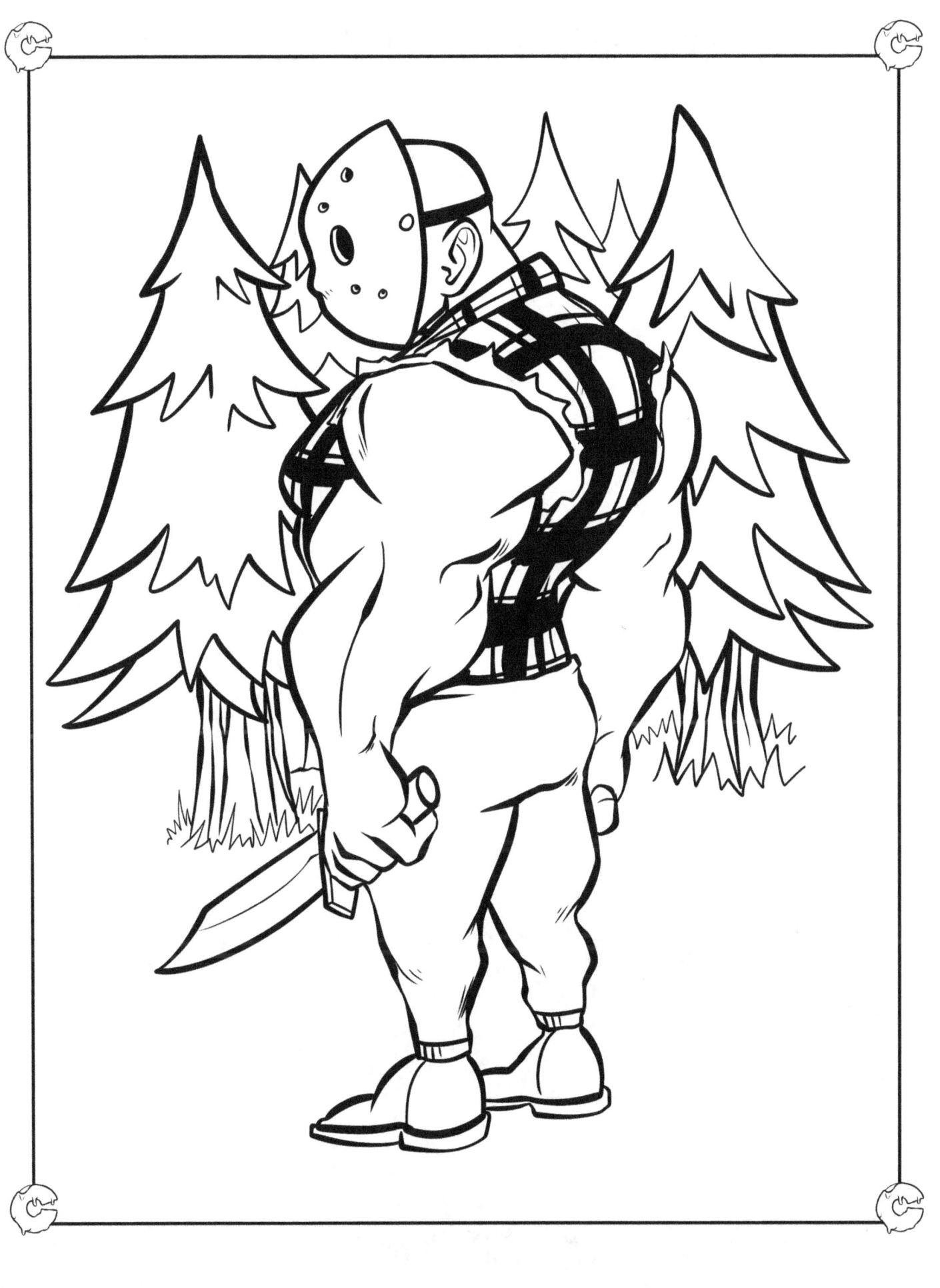

CREEPY CREATURE COLORING COLLECTION

BY JAKE PEREZ

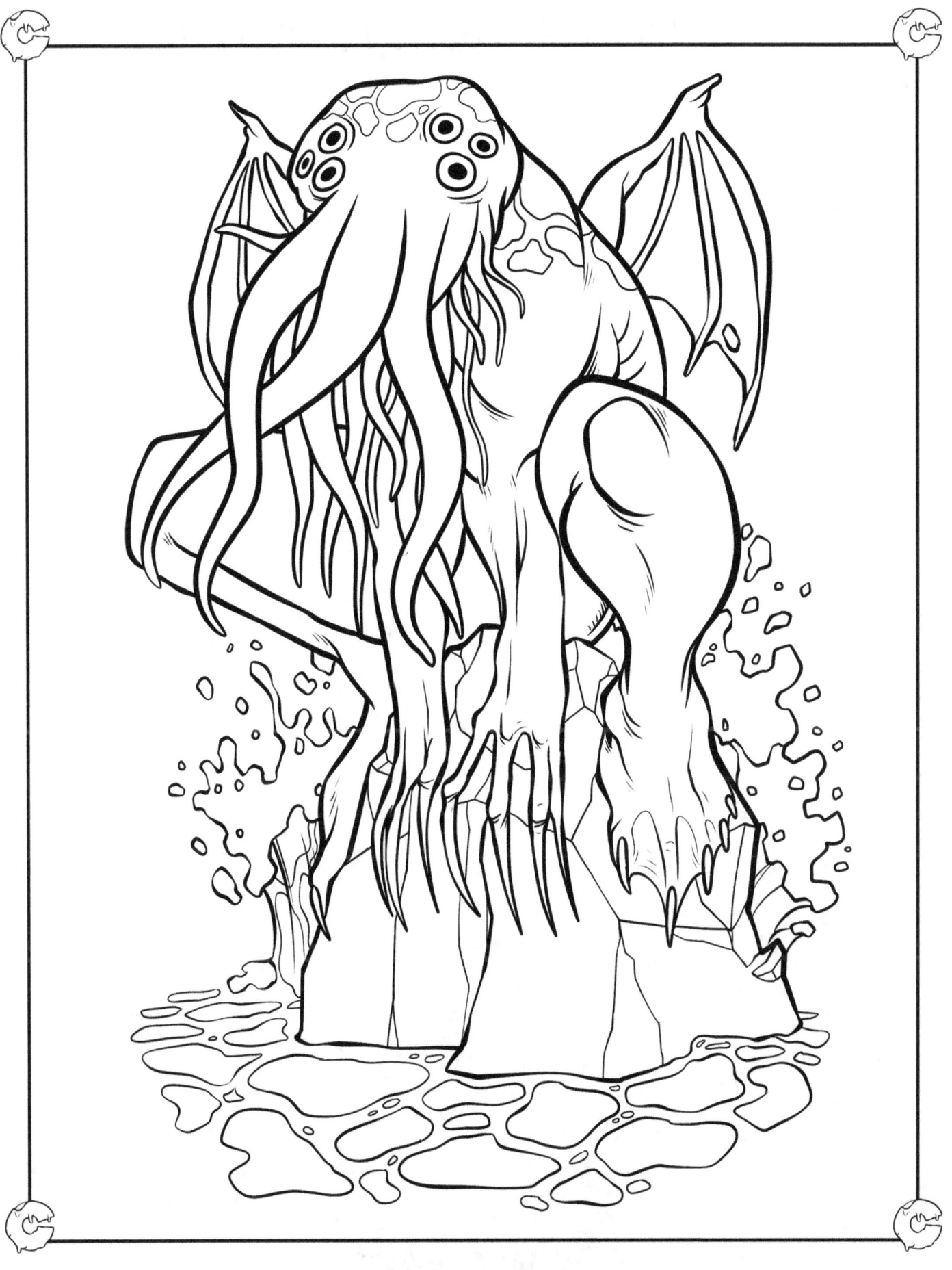

CREEPY CREATURE COLORING COLLECTION

BY JAKE PEREZ

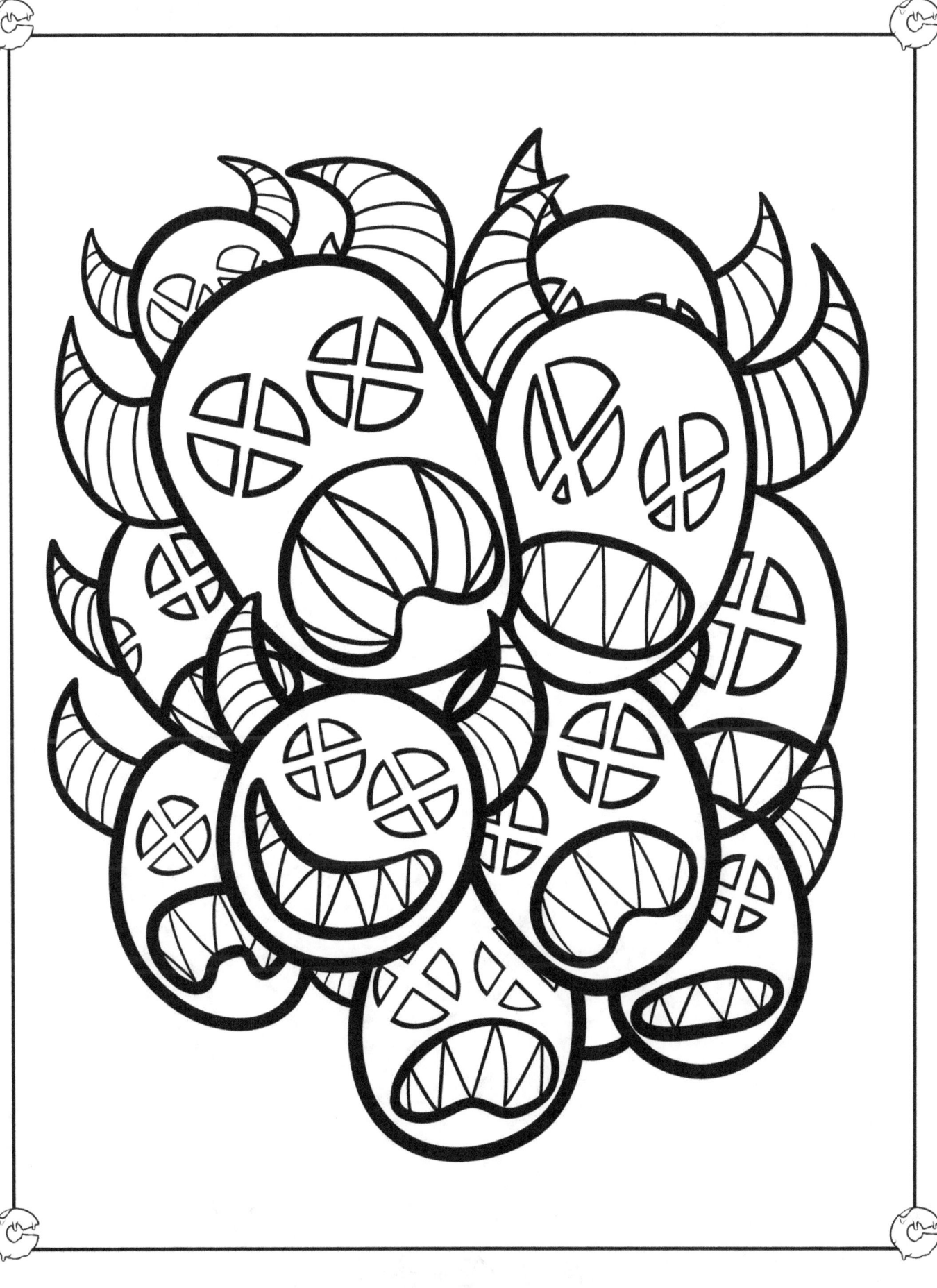

CREEPY CREATURE COLORING COLLECTION

BY JAKE PEREZ

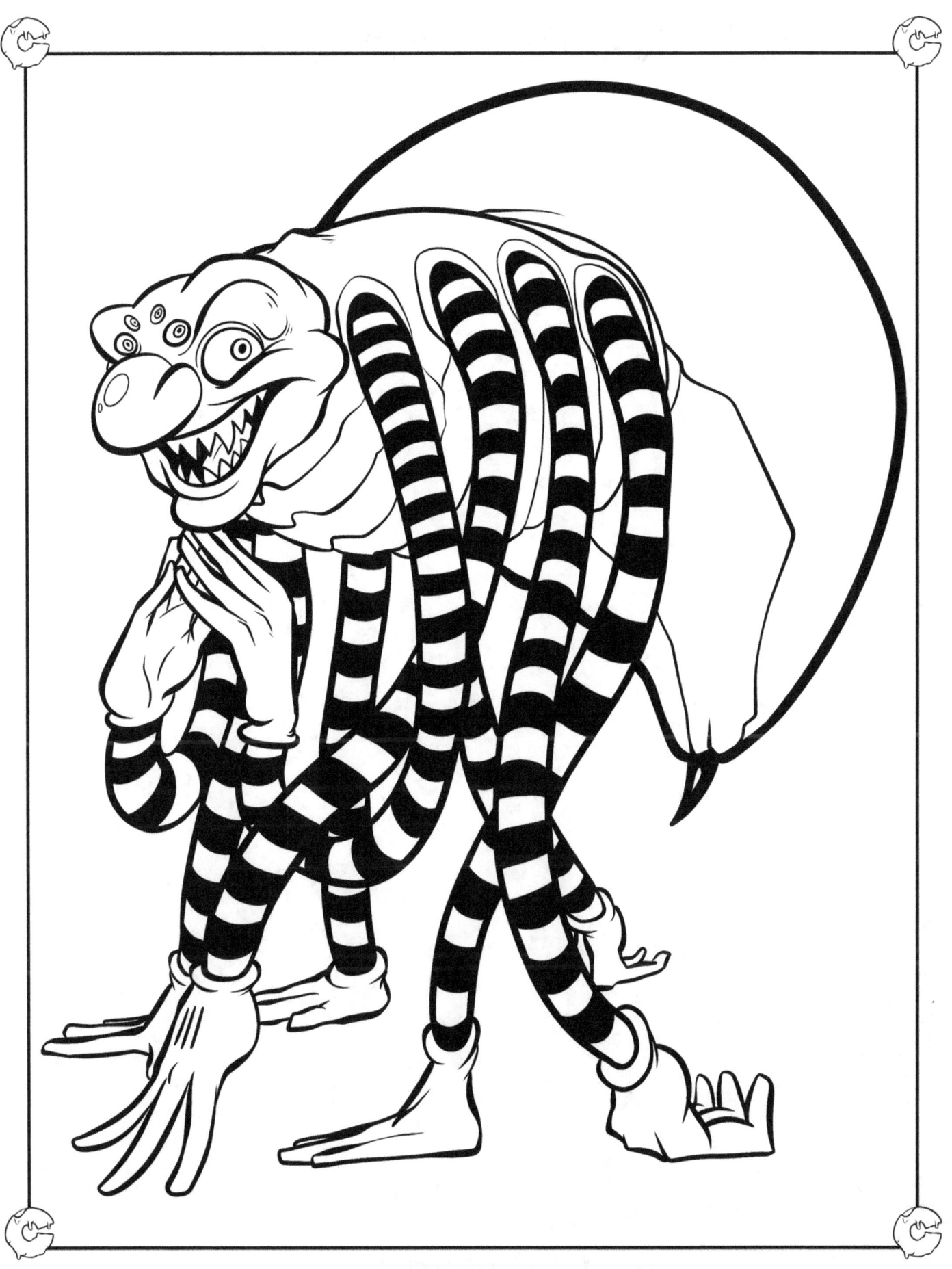

CREEPY CREATURE COLORING COLLECTION

BY JAKE PEREZ

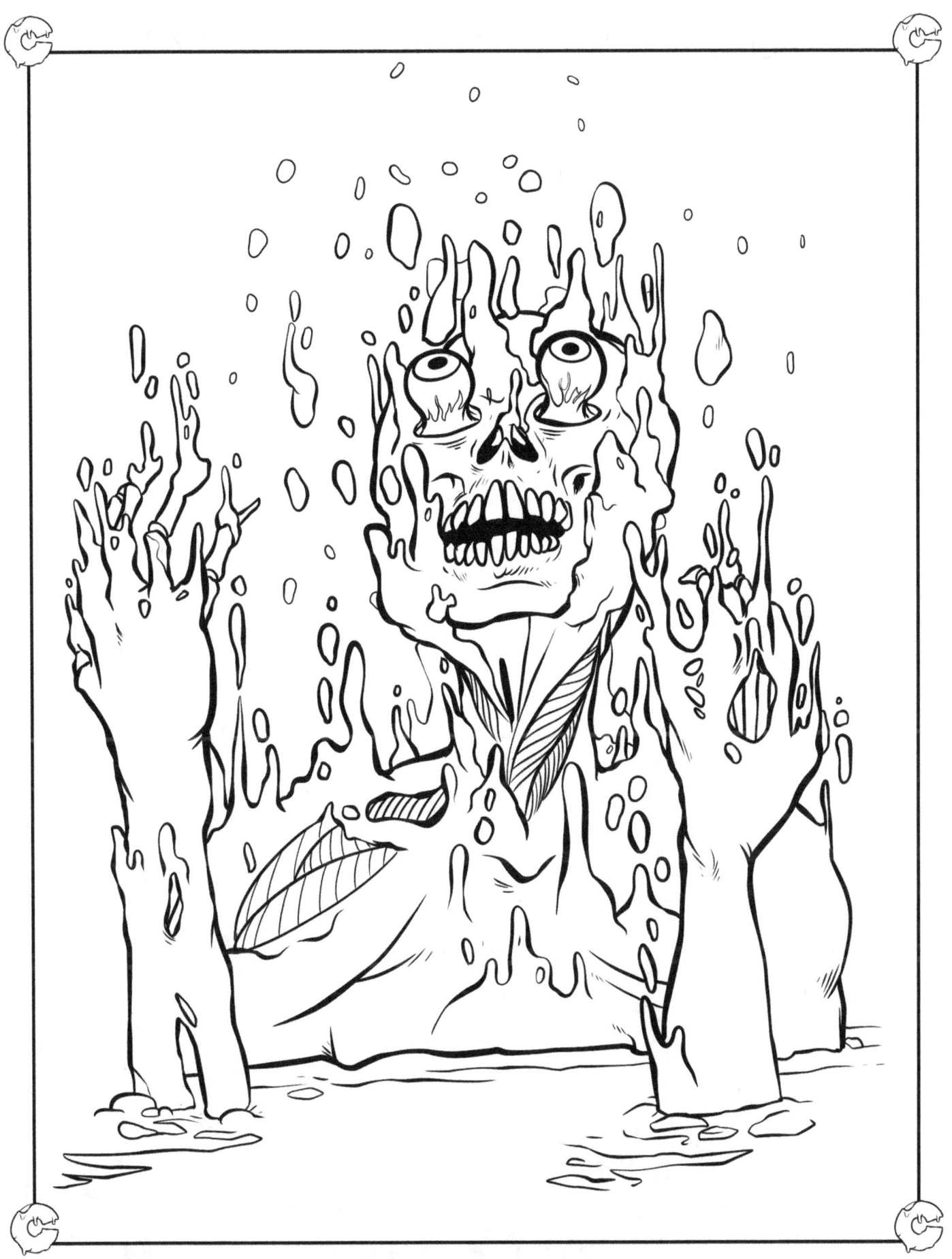

CREEPY CREATURE COLORING COLLECTION

BY JAKE PEREZ

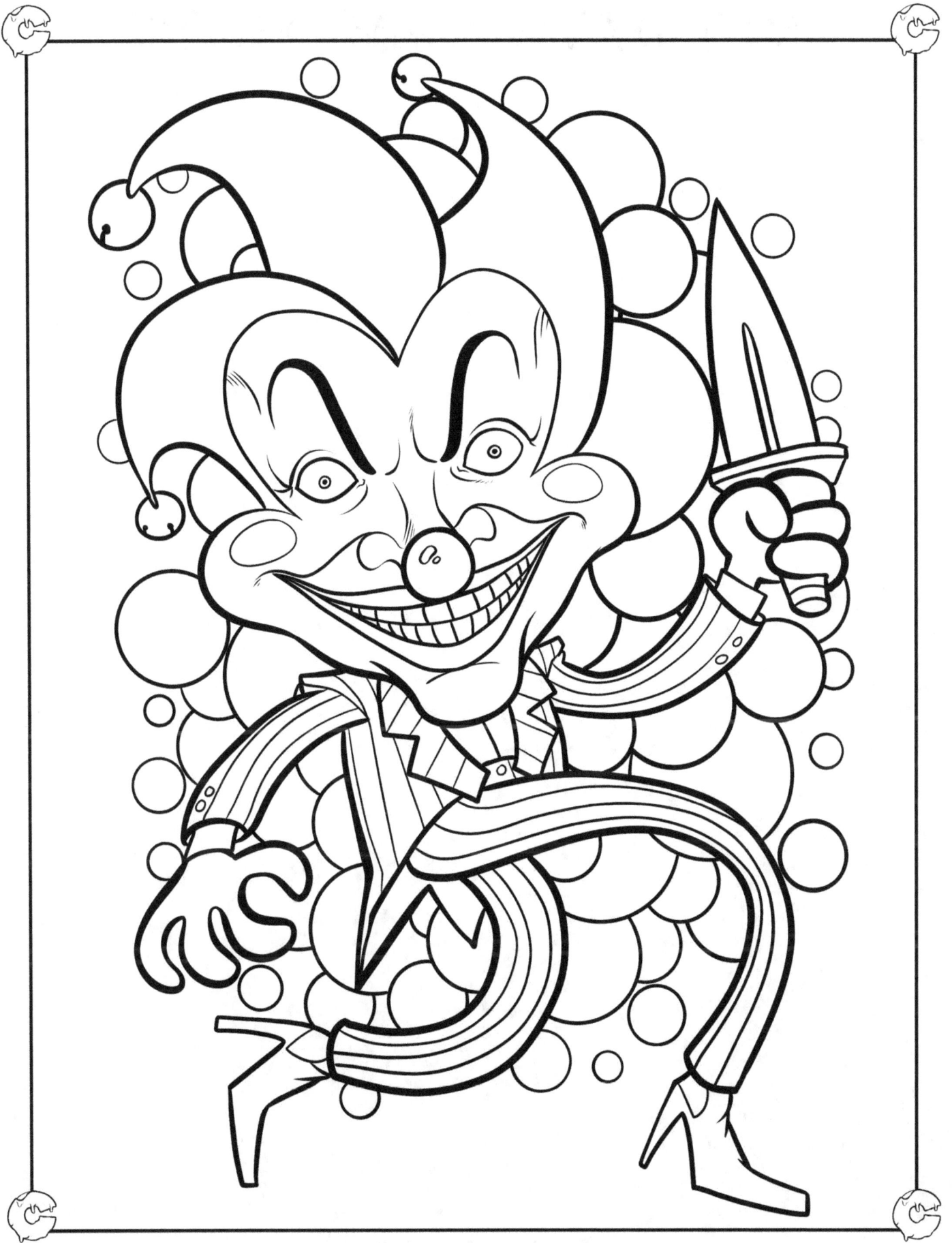

CREEPY CREATURE COLORING COLLECTION

BY JAKE PEREZ

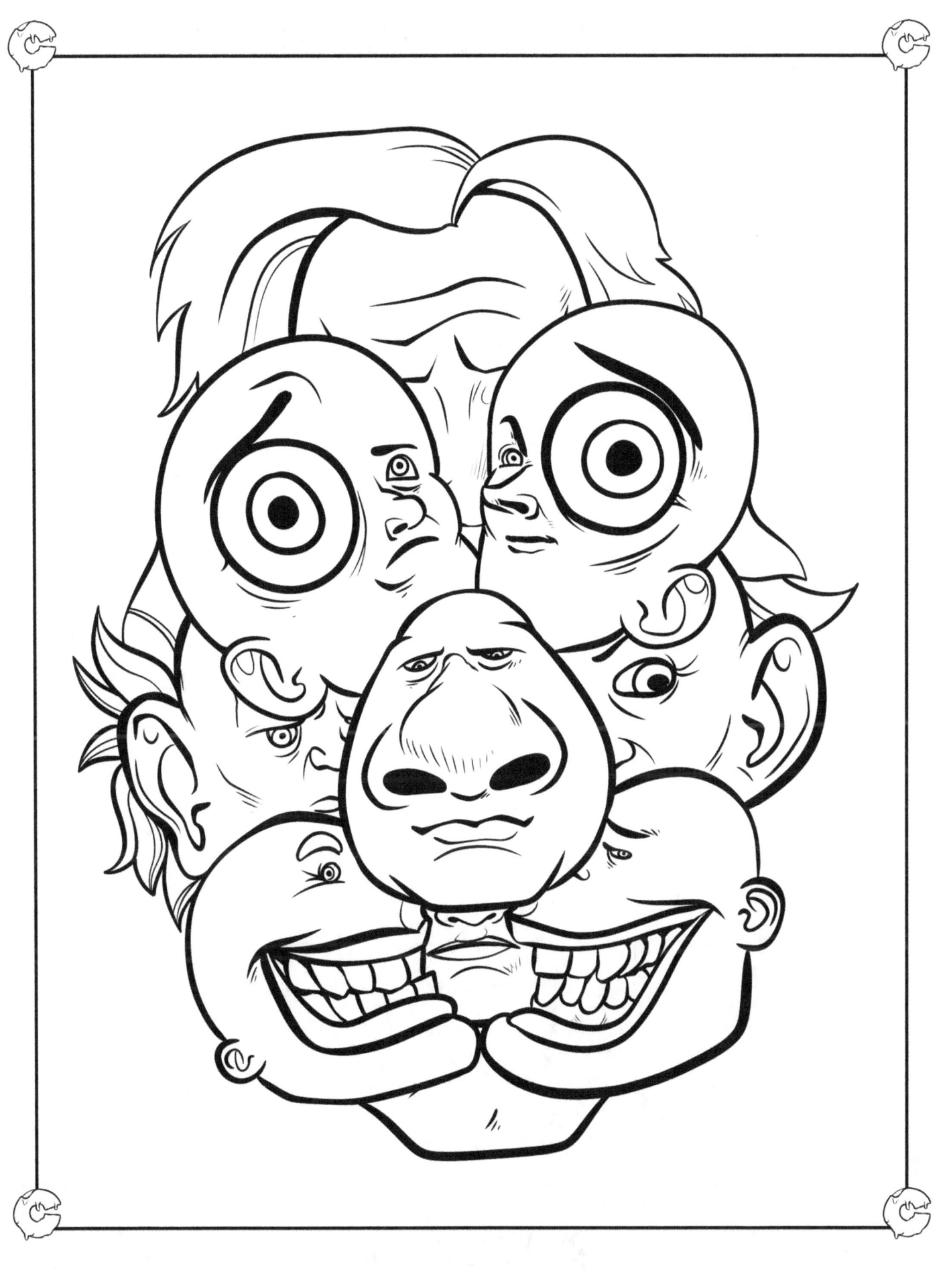

CREEPY CREATURE COLORING COLLECTION

BY JAKE PEREZ

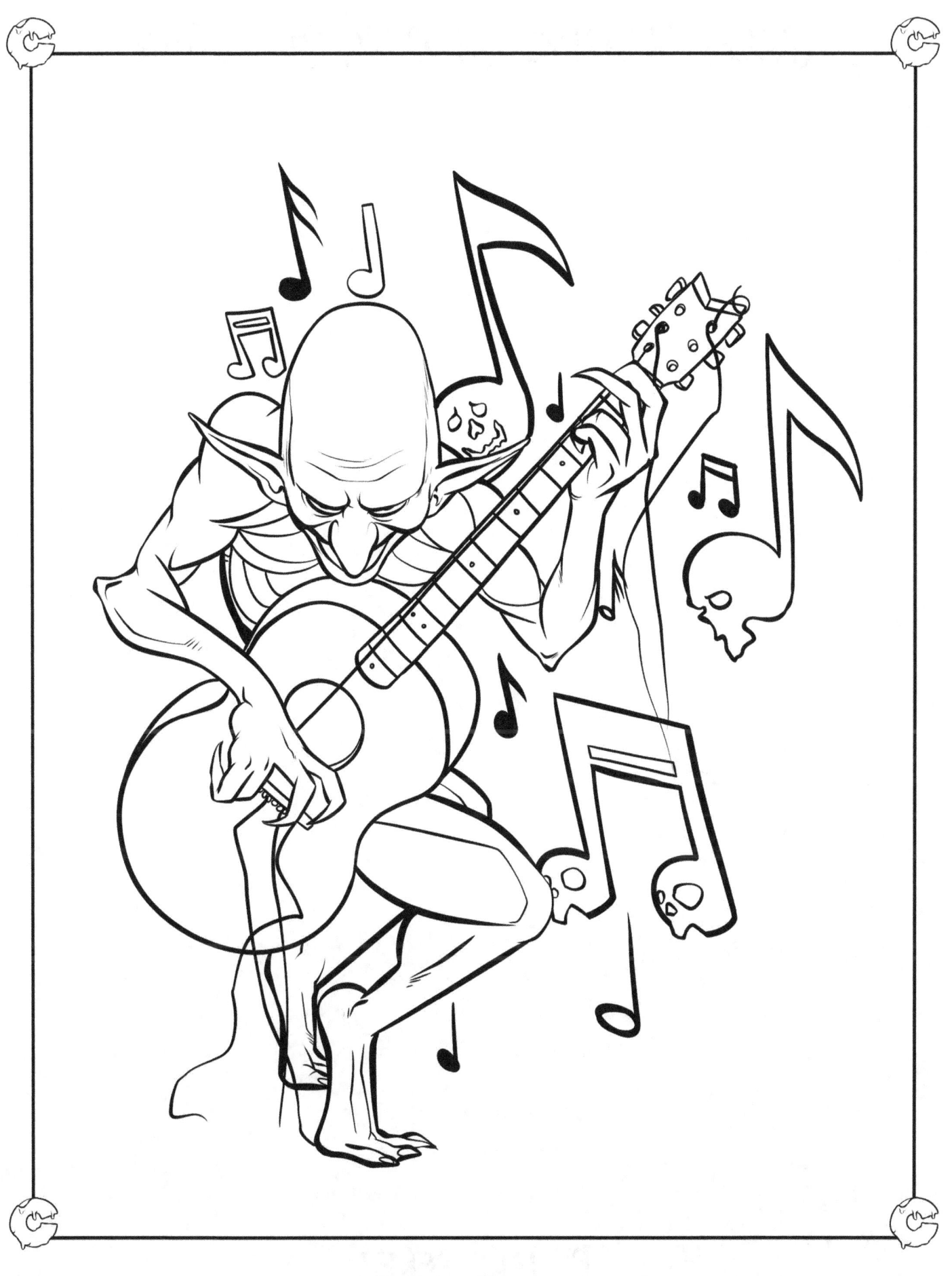

CREEPY CREATURE COLORING COLLECTION

BY JAKE PEREZ

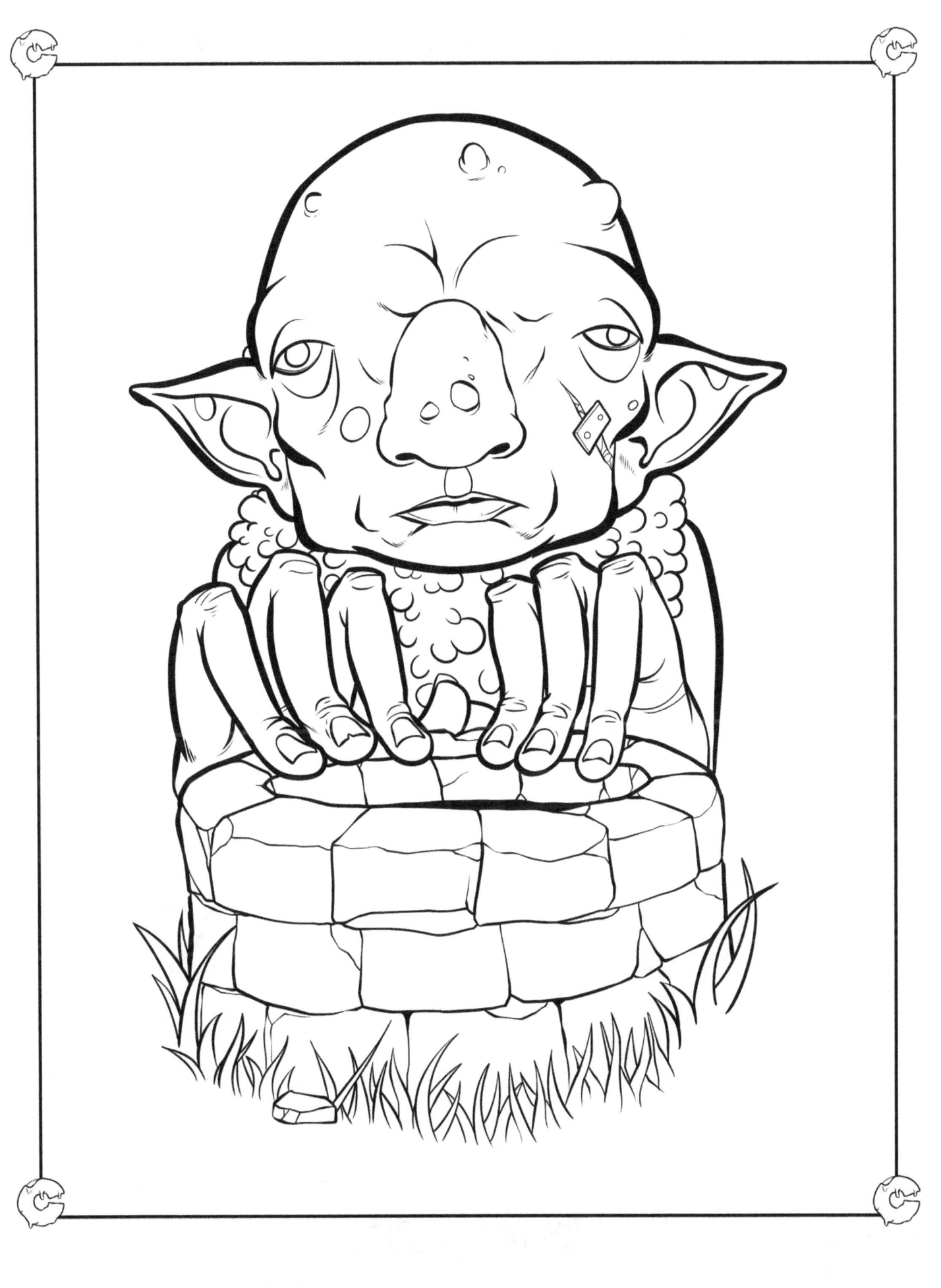

CREEPY CREATURE COLORING COLLECTION

BY JAKE PEREZ

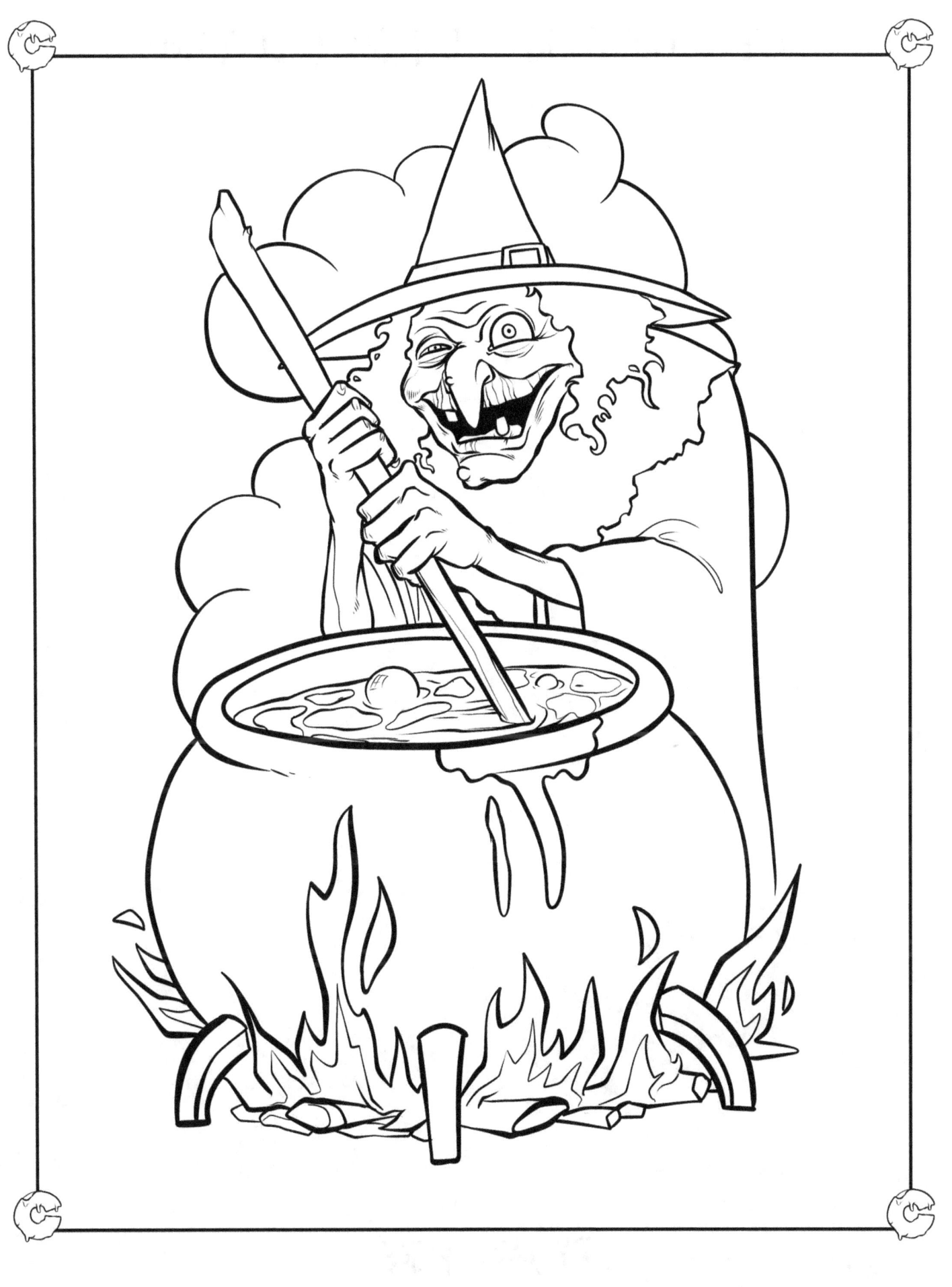

CREEPY CREATURE COLORING COLLECTION

BY JAKE PEREZ

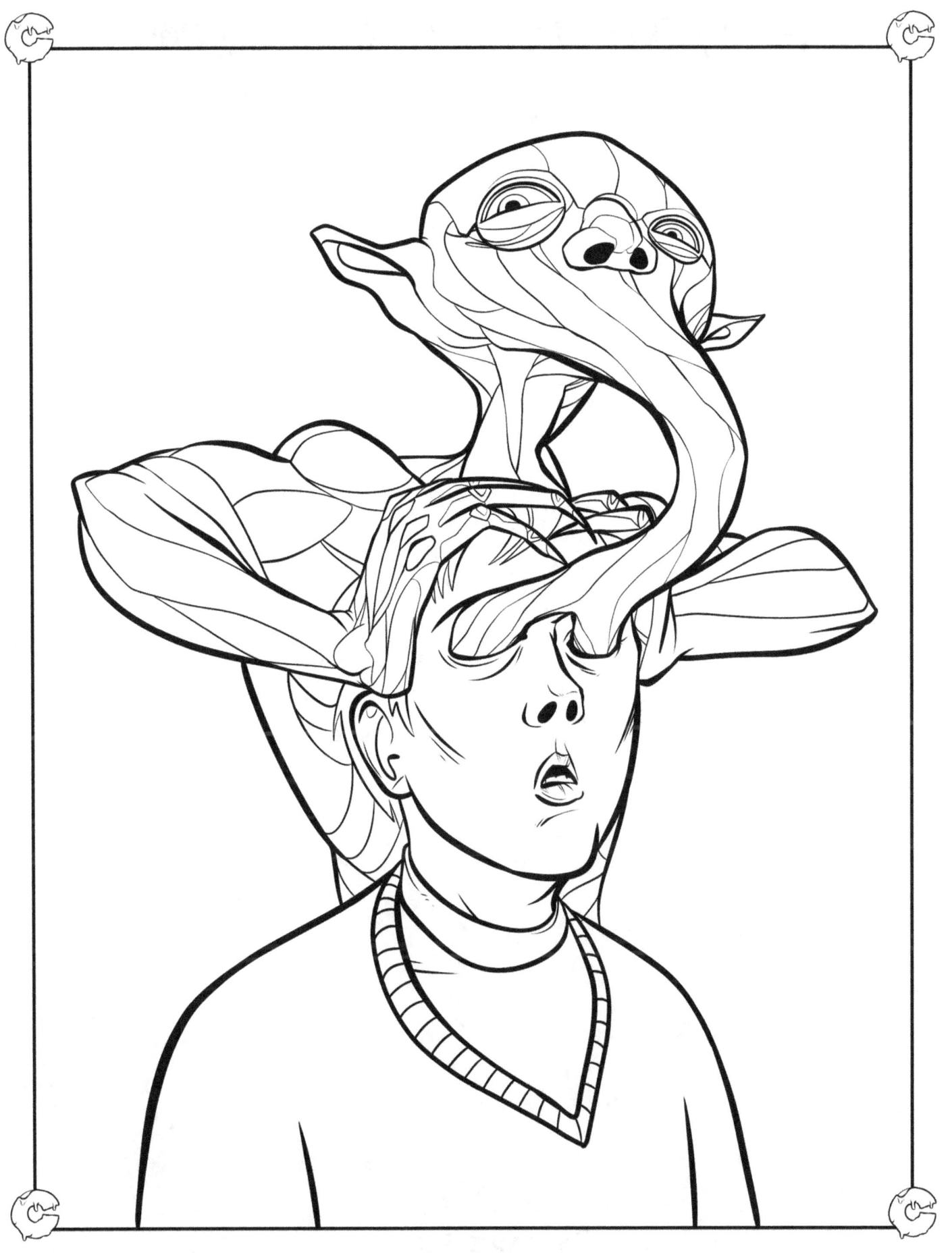

CREEPY CREATURE COLORING COLLECTION

BY JAKE PEREZ

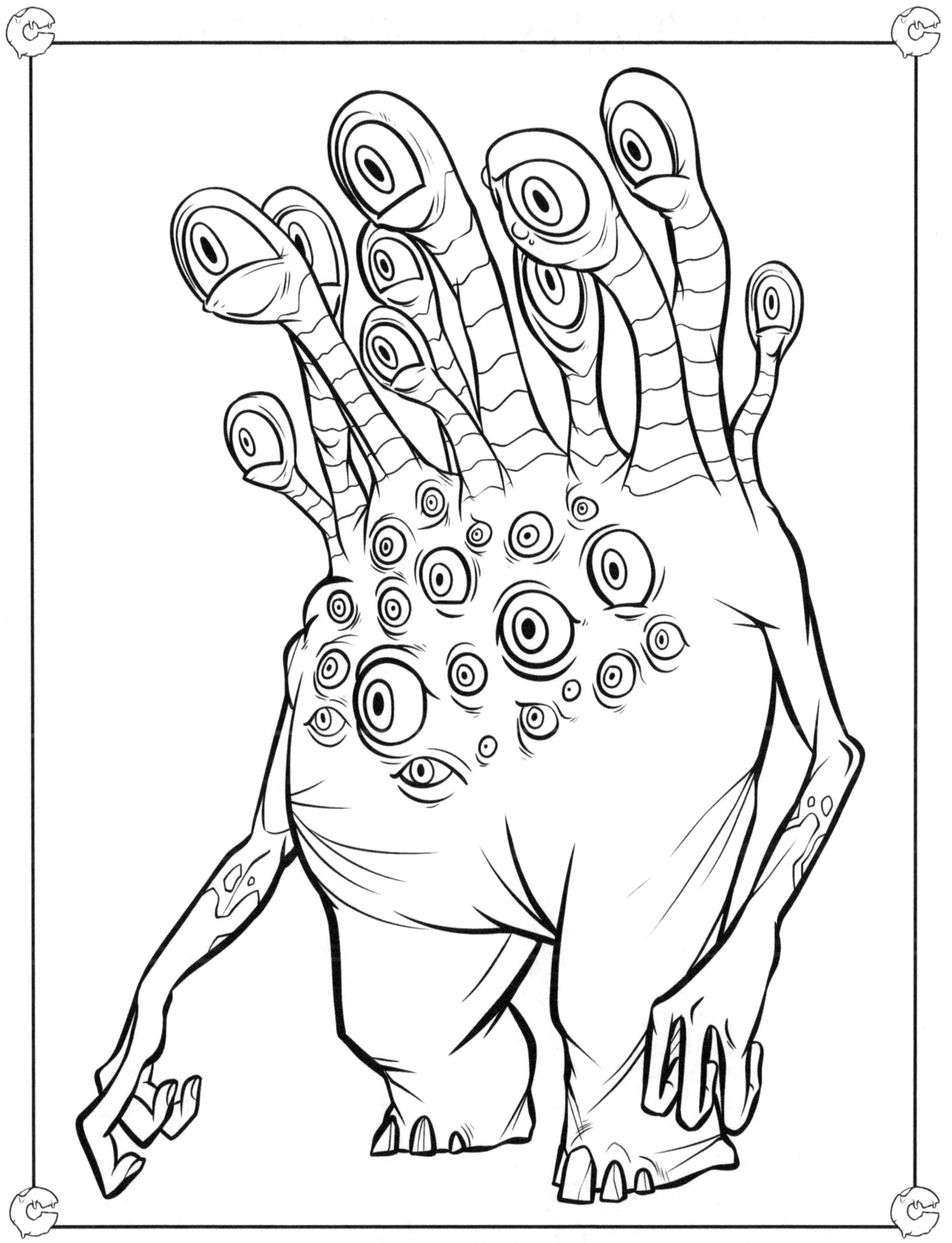

CREEPY CREATURE COLORING COLLECTION

BY JAKE PEREZ

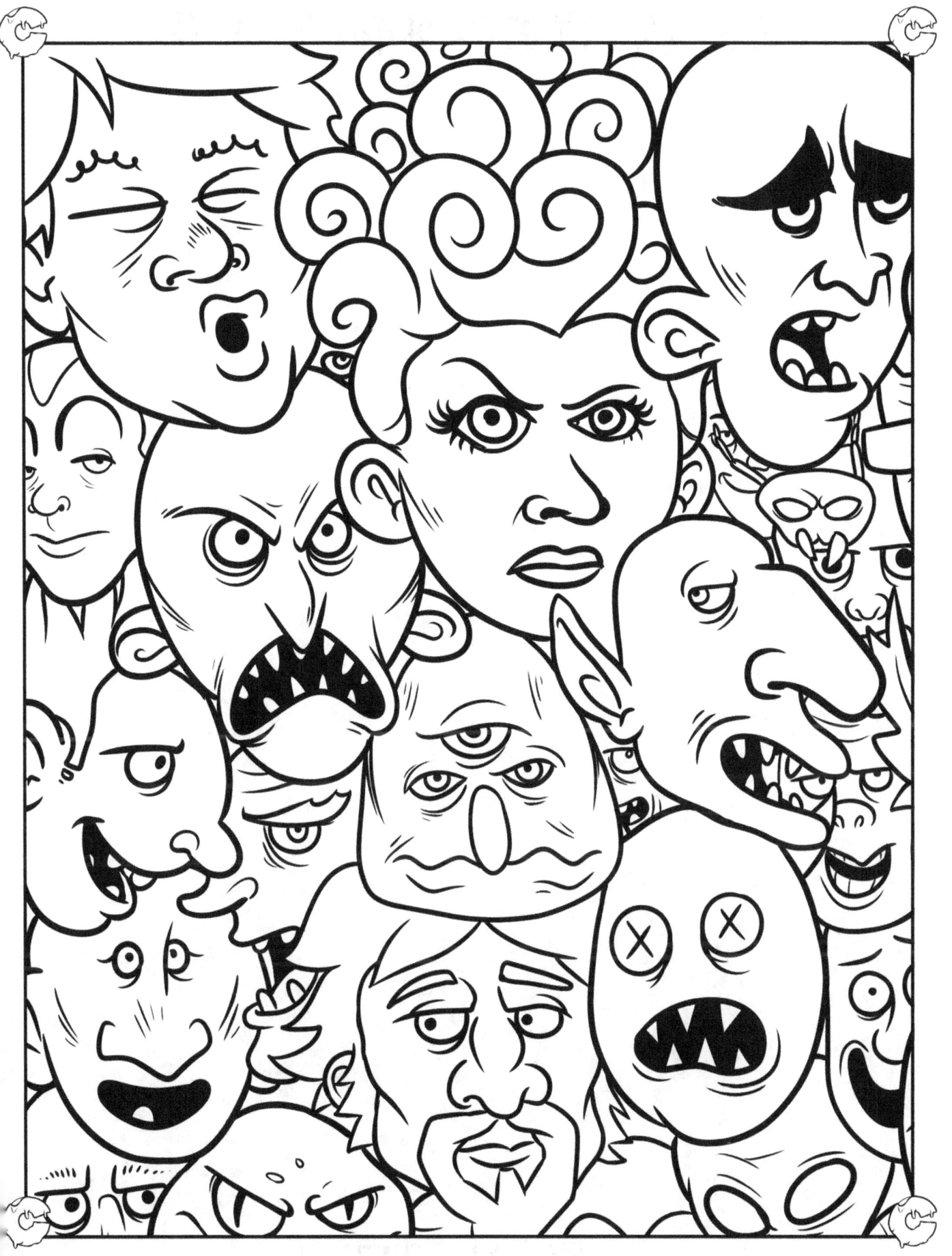

CREEPY CREATURE COLORING COLLECTION

BY JAKE PEREZ

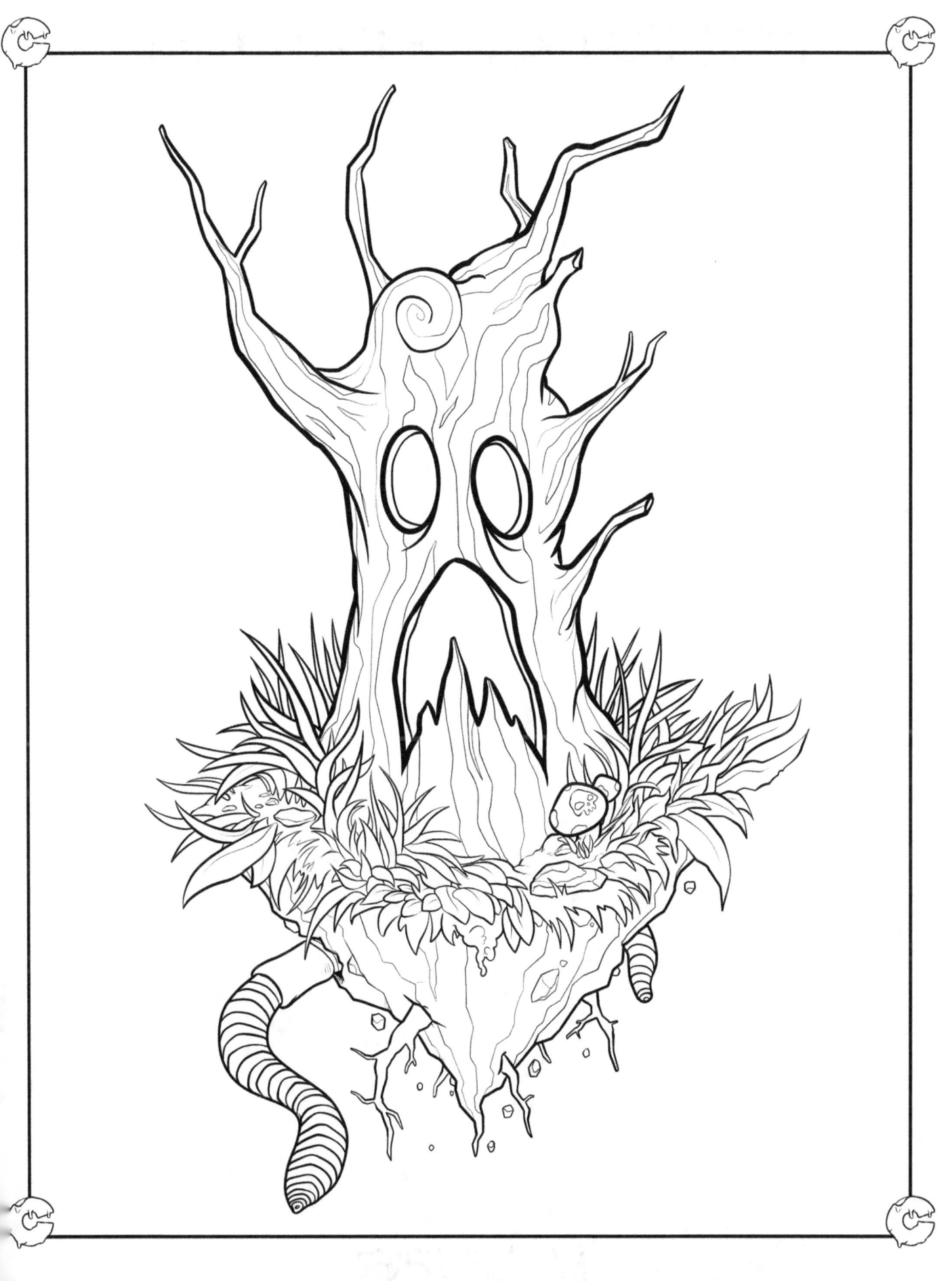

CREEPY CREATURE COLORING COLLECTION

BY JAKE PEREZ

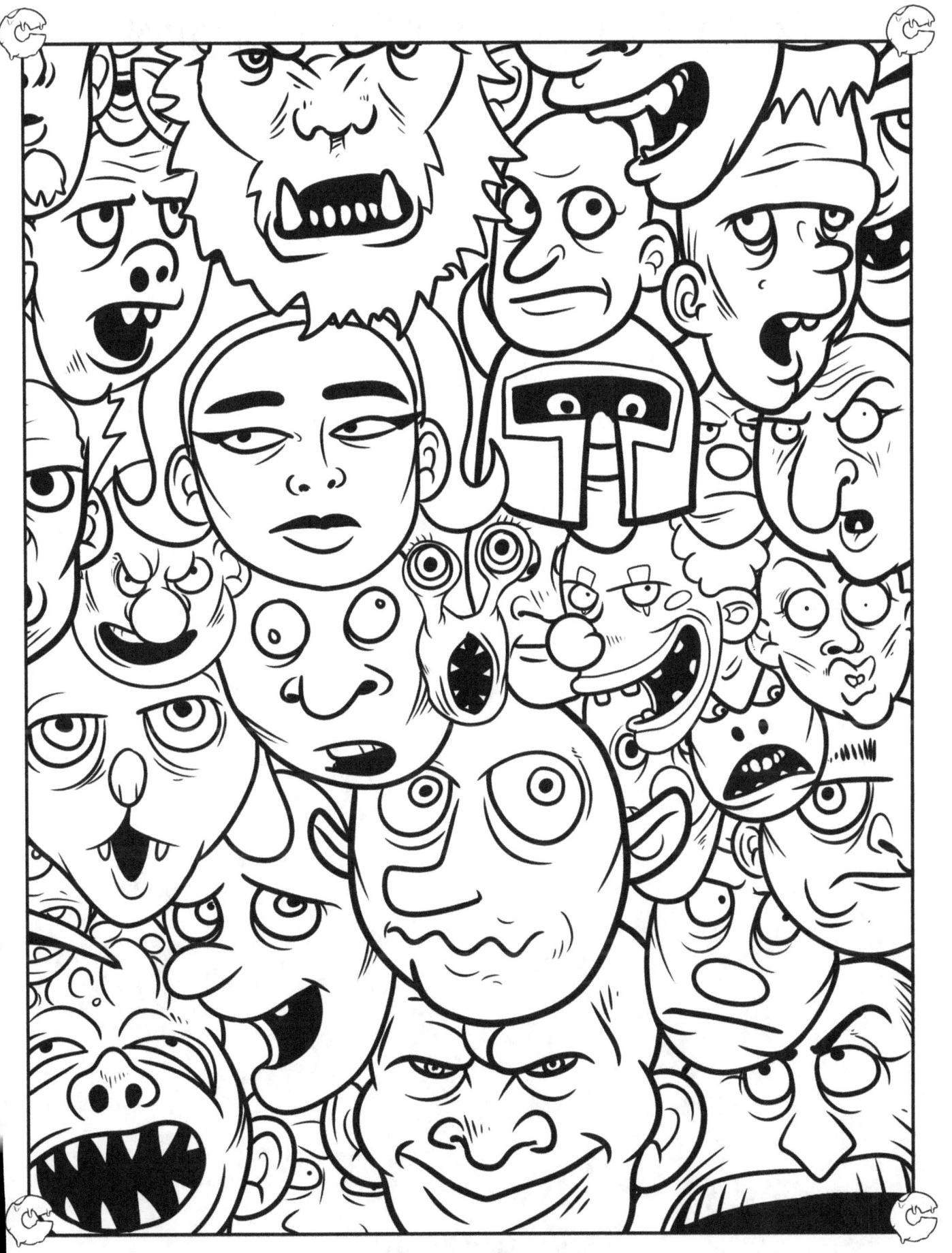

CREEPY CREATURE COLORING COLLECTION

BY JAKE PEREZ

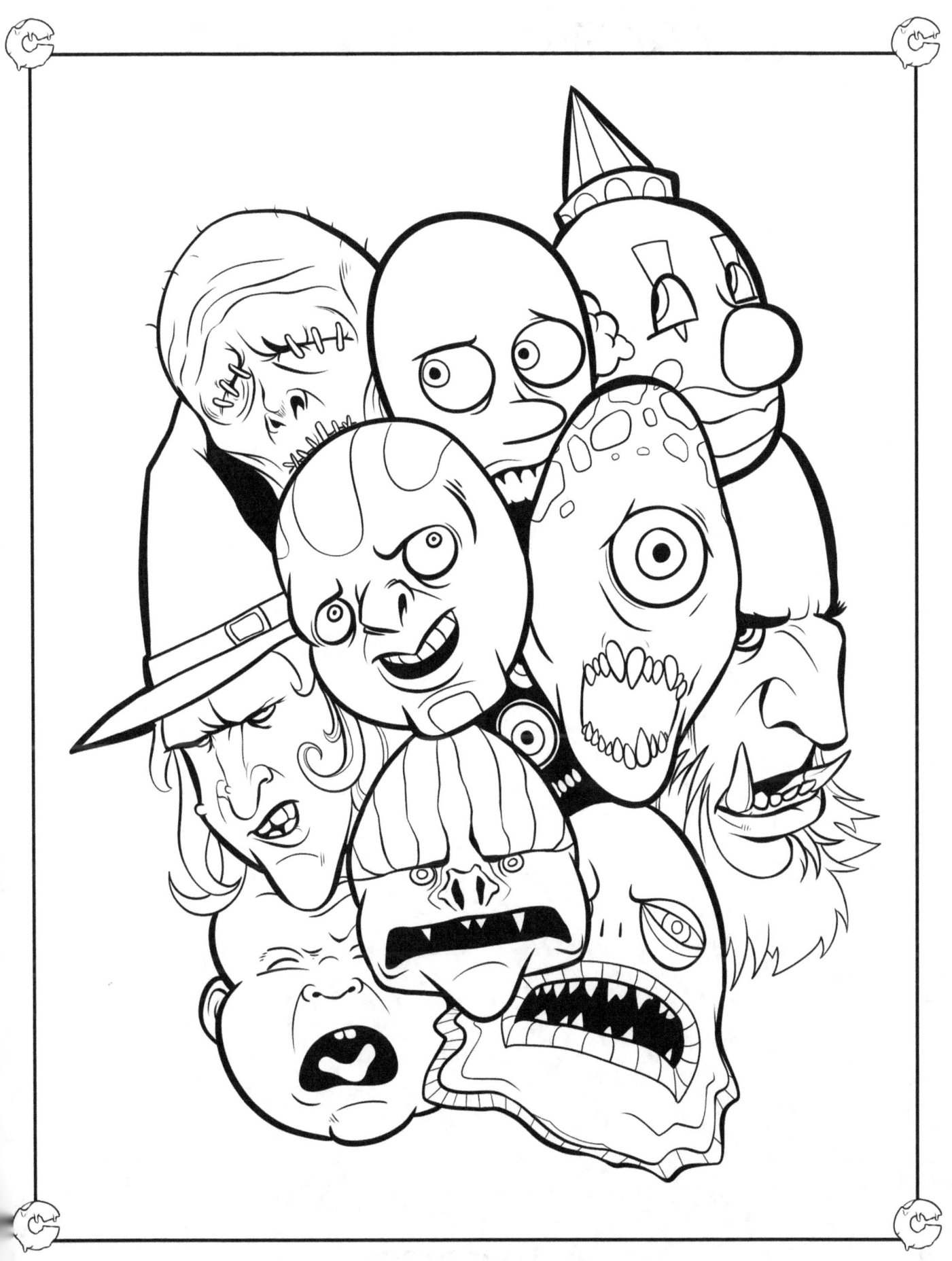

CREEPY CREATURE COLORING COLLECTION

BY JAKE PEREZ

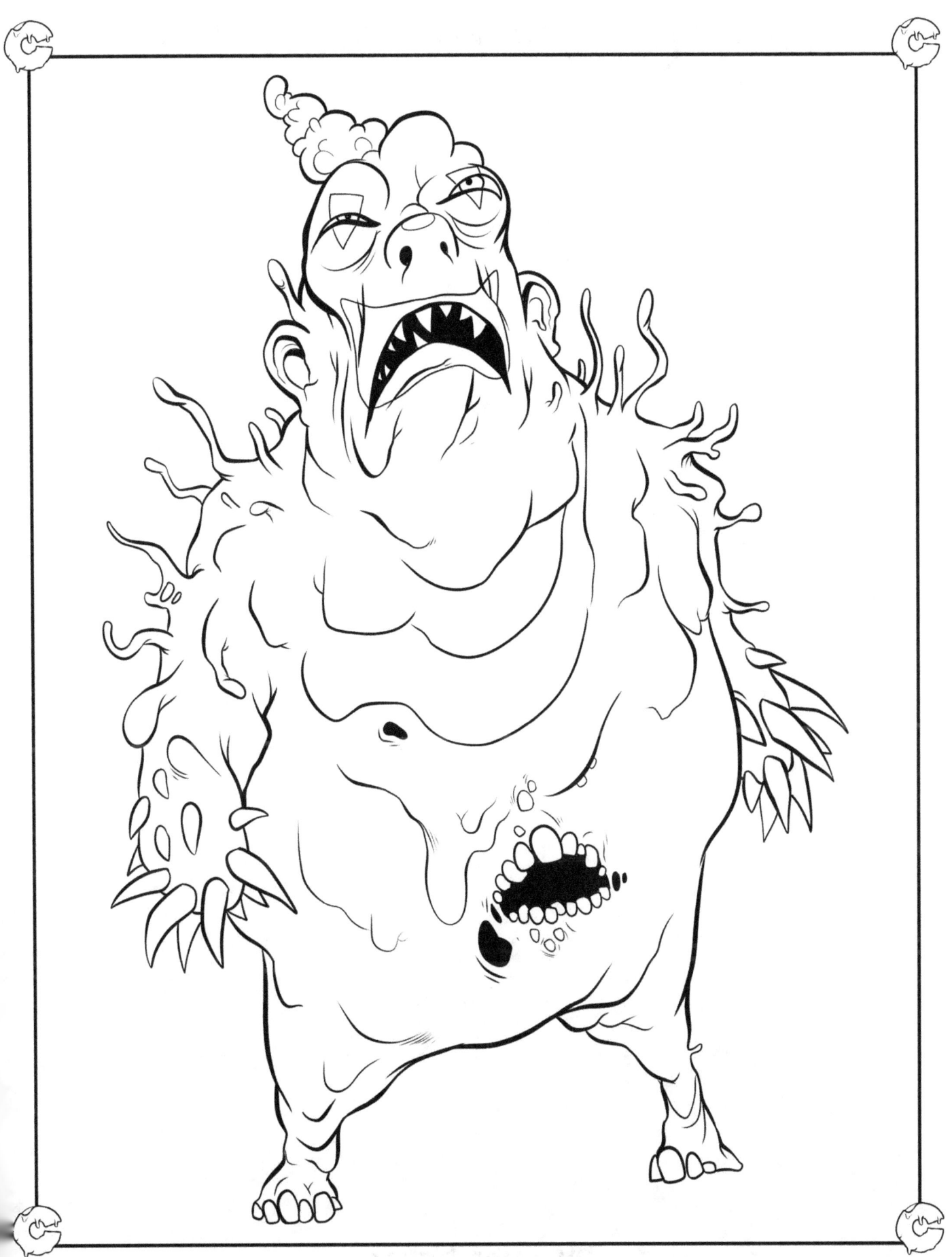

CREEPY CREATURE COLORING COLLECTION

BY JAKE PEREZ

www.ingramcontent.com/pod-product-compliance
Lightning Source LLC
Chambersburg PA
CBHW080502220526
45465CB00006B/2352